"WHO'S GONNA WATER MY TOMATOES?"

THE ACADEMY BOOK SERIES IN EDUCATION

Steven P. Jones and Eric C. Sheffield, *Editors*

The *Academy Book Series in Education* focuses serious attention on the often-missed nexus of educational theory and educational practice. The volumes in this series, both monographs and edited collections, consider theoretical, philosophical, historical, sociological, and other conceptual orientations in light of what those orientations can tell readers about successful classroom practice and sound educational policy. In this regard, the *Academy Series* aims to offer a wide array of themes including school reform, content-specific practice, contemporary problems in higher education, the impact of technology on teaching and learning, matters of diversity, and other essential contemporary issues in educational thought and practice.

BOOKS IN THE SERIES

Why Kids Love (and Hate) School: Reflections on Difference
by Steven Jones and Eric Sheffield (2018)
Why Kids Love (and Hate) School: Reflections on Practice
by Steven Jones and Eric Sheffield (2018)
A Case for Kindness: A New Look at the Teaching Ethic by Steve Broidy (2019)
Making Sense of Race in Education: Practices for Change in Difficult Times
edited by Jessica A. Heybach and Sharon Fraser-Burgess (2020)
John Dewey's Imaginative Vision of Teaching: Combining Theory and Practice
by Deron Boyles (2020)
Literary Imagination and Professional Knowledge: Using Literature in Teacher Education
edited by Jeff McLaughlin (2023)
What Do We Mean by That? Interrogating Familiar Expressions in Education
edited by Laura Rychly (2024)
"Who's Gonna Water My Tomatoes?": School Gardens, Kitchens, and the Search for Educational Authenticity by Michael Szolowicz (2024)
Diversifying the Educator Pipeline: Supporting Black Educators through Recruitment, Preparation, and Retention by Shaylyn Marks (2025)
A Preface to Educational Decision-Making (Working Title) by Steve Broidy (2025)

Steven P. Jones is a professor in the College of Education at Missouri State University and Executive Director of the Academy for Educational Studies. He is author of *Blame Teachers: The Emotional Reasons for Educational Reform*—a book that investigates how and why so many people try to justify educational change by deriding the efforts and effectiveness of our public school teachers. A former high school English teacher in Jefferson County, Colorado, Jones received his B.A. in English from the University of Denver, his M.A. in Educational Administration from the University of Colorado (Boulder), and his Ph.D. in Curriculum and Instruction from the University of Chicago.

Eric C. Sheffield is Professor and Department Chair of Educational Studies at Western Illinois University in Macomb. He is also founding editor of the Academy for Educational Studies' peer reviewed journal, *Critical Questions in Education*. A former English teacher in Putman County Florida, Sheffield received his B.A. in Philosophy from Illinois College, and his M.Ed (English Education) & Ph.D (Philosophy of Education) from the University of Florida.

The editors of the *Academy Book Series in Education* are interested in reviewing manuscripts and proposals for possible publication in the series. Scholars who wish to be considered should email their proposals, along with two sample chapters and current CVs, to the editors. For instructions and advice on preparing a prospectus, please refer to the Myers Education Press website at http://myersedpress.com/sites/stylus/MEP/Docs/Prospectus%20Guidelines%20MEP.pdf. You can send your material to:

Steven P. Jones and Eric C. Sheffield
academyedbooks@gmail.com

Advance Praise for

"WHO'S GONNA WATER MY TOMATOES?"
School Gardens, Kitchens, and the Search for Educational Authenticity

"*Who's Gonna Water My Tomatoes?*" is a must read for those in education exploring beyond traditional models. With deep insights into Edible Education, the author reveals the transformative impact of food literacy programs on students. Drawing from John Dewey's timeless philosophy, the book illustrates how education can jump conventional boundaries, empowering children with essential life skills. A compelling blend of history and practical wisdom, it's a testament to the profound benefits of shaping future generations through experiential learning while inspiring them to have a healthy relationship with the food they eat.

—DYLAN WILSON,
EXECUTIVE DIRECTOR, BUENA VISTA EDIBLE SCHOOLYARD

The author has masterfully captured the very essence of the Edible Schoolyard, intertwining the experiential, hands-on journeys of students from the garden to the kitchen. The book details the transformative process of planting, nurturing, and harvesting, and aligning with the essential culinary experiences where wholesome, tasty recipes are prepared and savored. This dynamic and seasonal seed-to-table cycle is where true learning occurs, as knowledge and experiences in the garden translate into lasting, healthy eating behaviors and practices. Through the pages of this book, readers will witness a transfer of wisdom and practical skills, fostering a new generation of mindful eaters and gardeners. This unique combination not only educates but inspires, making the book a must-read for anyone passionate about sustainable living and the profound impact of experiential learning.

—RJ VALENTINO,
PRESIDENT, GRIMM FAMILY EDUCATION FOUNDATION

Michael Szolowicz's volume provides a theoretically grounded account of school gardens and kitchens amidst multiple, complex influences on public education, including externalized accountability, pressures for curriculum standardization, climate change, and a pandemic among others. There has been a growing interest in school gardens and kitchens in recent years. Szolowicz's volume is unique in that it builds upon historical lessons from John Dewey to demonstrate how students learn from experience with food as a source of nourishment and community. The book is well grounded theoretically with examples that engage the reader in possibilities for authentic education beyond individualism and standardization.

—DR. ROSE M. YLIMAKI,
DEL AND JEWELL LEWIS ENDOWED CHAIR IN EDUCATIONAL LEADERSHIP
NORTHERN ARIZONA UNIVERSITY

Who's Gonna Water My Tomatoes: School Gardens, Kitchens, and the Search for Educational Authenticity is a rich resource that provides a healthy (*literally*) food for thought for educators to move students from being *full of skills* to *skillful*. Showing himself to be a thorough student of John Dewey and others, Szolowicz, an experienced researcher-practitioner, aptly provides a rich menu for learning-hungry students, innovation-driven teachers, curriculum designers, transformative leaders to cultivate authentic place-based learning at schools. Readers will particularly find effective pedagogical strategies that can reify ecological, scientific and all literacy skills while producing healthy fruits for the benefit of everyone at schools and communities at large. Grounded in prominent epistemologies and rich research, the book serves as a didactic and practical recipe and actionable manual that takes holistic learning-teaching and empowerment to the higher levels. It is a *must-read* volume!

—Mahmoud Suleiman, Ph.D.
Interim Director, Doctoral Program in Educational Leadership
California State University, Bakersfield

In *Who's Gonna Water My Tomatoes?* Szolowicz clearly articulates "the why" and "the how" as it applies to the need for all schools to create edible schoolyards. Furthermore, and perhaps most importantly, Szolowicz shares exactly how schools can aim to incorporate edible school-yards in the process of educating their students.

—Dr. Denver J. Fowler,
Associate Dean, Graduate and Undergraduate Studies,
California State University, Bakersfield

"WHO'S GONNA WATER MY TOMATOES?"

School Gardens, Kitchens, and the Search for Educational Authenticity

By Michael A. Szolowicz

Myers Education Press

GORHAM, MAINE

Myers Education Press

Published by Myers Education Press, LLC
P.O. Box 424 Gorham, ME 04038

Myers Education Press is an academic publisher specializing in books, e-books, and digital content in the field of education. All of our books are subjected to a rigorous peer-review process and produced in compliance with the standards of the Council on Library and Information Resources.

Library of Congress Cataloging-in-Publication Data available from Library of Congress.

13-digit ISBN 978-1-9755-0614-8 (paperback)
13-digit ISBN 978-1-9755-0615-5 (library networkable e-edition)
13-digit ISBN 978-1-9755-0616-2 (consumer e-edition)

Printed in the United States of America.

All first editions printed on acid-free paper that meets the American National Standards Institute Z39-48 standard.

Books published by Myers Education Press may be purchased at special quantity discount rates for groups, workshops, training organizations, and classroom usage. Please call our customer service department at 1-800-232-0223 for details.

Cover design by Teresa Lagrange.

Visit us on the web at **www.myersedpress.com** to browse our complete list of titles.

TABLE OF CONTENTS

LIST OF TABLES

ACKNOWLEDGMENTS

THE JOURNEY OF A book from its conceptual seed to its finished fruit, akin to a ripe, harvested tomato, is a communal effort. I extend my heartfelt gratitude to Dr. John Stark, the now-retired director of the Doctoral Program in Educational Leadership at California State University, Bakersfield. Dr. Stark initiated this project and provided invaluable guidance and support throughout the research and editing phases. I also want to acknowledge Barbara Grimm Marshall for her visionary leadership and dedication to integrating innovative Edible Schoolyard programs into the educational model. The collaboration and support of the Grimm Family Education Foundation were instrumental in bringing this book to life. Finally, my sincere thanks to Steven P. Jones of the Academy for Educational Studies and the Critical Questions in Education Conferences. His encouragement to expand this work into book form and his suggestions for linking it with Dewey's philosophy were key contributions to this endeavor.

FOREWORD

Dr. John Stark

World competition is heating up, with countries creating more trade barriers to insulate their economies. What this ultimately means is that each country is going to be relying more and more on the resources and capabilities within its own borders. Given this, in looking at the United States, while still enjoying significant advantages in natural resources, the country is losing ground in the development of its human resources, especially with respect to education. Recent findings of learning skills in math, science, and reading highlight that the U.S. is actually falling behind other major economies (e.g., University of Kansas blog, 2023). COVID-19 certainly didn't help things, as math and reading scores actually dropped, and gaps between students at the top and bottom increased (Kuhfeld et al., 2022). The ongoing problem with this drop during the pandemic is that things are not bouncing back (Ross, 2024). The question, then, is how best to reverse the trend and get U.S. education back on track to support our competitive posture.

As this book will tell you, this question of how best to educate our kids is not a new one. In fact, over 100 years ago, John Dewey (1915/2010) held very similar concerns and determined that the key to educational improvement involved enticing the students to actively engage in the process. However, in looking at the current focus on institutional testing and the massive amounts of time spent drilling kids in test preparation, it is hard to see how kids would be drawn into such a process, find interest in it, and fully engage. It is easy to remember our own education and asking such questions as when we would ever need to use fractions (or name your particular bane in mathematics) or why we needed to read so much. In dealing with such natural resistance, it is mystifying that we would try to force learning in such a mechanical way. And, given what is at stake, we need education to be successful.

In this book, Dr. Szolowicz offers an alternative, one that Dewey (1915/2010) supported all those years ago: school edible garden programs. In a nutshell, what is proposed is that students be involved in planting, cultivating, harvesting, and then preparing garden output to eat. In this process, the students are exposed to practical lessons, using the very concepts that they may eschew back in the typical classroom (think about using fractions in baking, for example—there is a very funny and practical story along these lines in the book). The point is that students experience the need for the knowledge and skills being learned.

The result of this experience is not just a matter of students having fun. This book is backed up by actual research showing that there are positive educational outcomes to be had. This is not surprising, as the students are more motivated via this approach to learn because they can see why they need the knowledge and skills. Also, it seems that the learning could be more robust, as the students get to practice using what they have learned. We have known for years that retention of information is only 10% to 20% if we read or see audio-visual (think PowerPoint) presentations of information, but nearer to 75% if we use the information in activities (NTL Institute, 2020). Therefore, applied activities, such as edible schoolyards, have the potential to enhance the learning experience and help get our educational system back on track.

This book not only makes the case for the value of the edible schoolyards and supports the case with research, but there is also guidance on how you can start such a program for your own school. The path for such programs can start very small, by simply beginning with plants growing on the windowsills in classrooms. This can then be ramped up to planters outside the school building and can eventually be expanded to dedicated space for a full garden. (Examples in the book include gardens reaching an acre in size and providing a key focal point for the entire school facility.) The point is that this book can get you started on providing your students with the opportunity to more fully engage in their own educational process.

In returning to where I began, the U.S. educational system is simply not headed in a productive direction, and the country cannot afford the likely outcomes of staying the course in this direction. We need to make a change. This book offers a real option for taking things in a different direction and obtaining the outcomes that we sorely need. I recommend it to you for consideration and wish you the best in your efforts to maximize the learning outcomes for your students.

References

Dewey, J. (2010). *The school and society and the child and the curriculum* (2nd ed.). Digireads.com publishing. (Original work published 1915)

Kuhfeld, M., Soland, J., Lewis, K., & Morton, E. (2022). *The pandemic has devastating impacts on learning. What will it take to catch up?* The Brookings Institute. https://www.brookings.edu/articles/the-pandemic-has-had-devastating-impacts-on-learning-what-will-it-take-to-help-students-catch-up/

NTL Institute for Applied Behavioral Sciences. (2020). The learning ladder. In D.A. Whetten & K.S. Cameron (Eds.), *Developing Management Skills* (10th ed., pp. 445–485). Pearson.

Ross, E. (2024). *Despite progress, achievement gaps persist during recovery from pandemic.* Harvard Graduate School of Education. https://www.gse.harvard.edu/ideas/news/24/01/despite-progress-achievement-gaps-persist-during-recovery-pandemic

University of Kansas. (2023). *How USA education measures up worldwide.* https://educationonline.ku.edu/community/how-usa-education-measures-up-worldwide

CHAPTER ONE

INTRODUCTION

WE ARRIVED AT THE garden early on a crisp spring morning. The chill in the air made the jeans and jackets my son and I wore a good idea, but the bright sun promised a warm day ahead. Regardless, we were both happy to be out of the house, away from computer screens and breathing fresh air without masks. Well, at least I was happy about these things. I wasn't sure Josh was too thrilled to be away from the computer and phone screens he had become so accustomed to during the waning pandemic. I also wasn't sure how he would react to the labor ahead of us, but he did need volunteer hours for the National Honor Society, while I was pleased to experience the gardens I had been studying during the past few months.

We parked in the almost empty school lot. The elementary school associated with this edible schoolyard was on spring break, but the dedicated garden staff was on duty, attending to various maintenance and future lesson preparation needs. We met them near the kitchen building after wandering along the path beside fruit trees, neatly planted rows of various leafy vegetables, and shiny waist-high metal horse troughs filled with fragrant herbs. Fresh mulch filled the spaces between plantings and provided a fresh, almost woodsy aroma in addition to contributing to the neatly groomed garden aesthetic. A grapevine grew on a trellis along one of the pathways branching off from the one we walked. Several neatly constructed buildings, including a greenhouse, rose on the other side of the acre-sized property, as did the olive trees that formed the garden's eastern border. In the distance, the sound of clucking chickens pecking the ground for breakfast emerged softly.

We met the garden staff near the kitchen building but then moved to the shade of a ramada structure in the heart of the garden. Constructed of wood trimmed from local trees, the open-air structure included benches with seating for about thirty students so that they could keep in the shade during class meetings in the garden. Passing through the ramada, we walked past a sundial built into the ground and toward one of the small buildings which turned out to be a shed filled with tools. The garden staff explained that all the garden tools were real and that there were no toys. My mind flashed back with greater understanding to one of our student survey results in which some students had named working with the various tools as their favorite part of the garden experience, and surveyed the shovels, pitchforks, shears, saws, and other tools with fresh appreciation.

We chose pitchforks with smooth wooden handles and light green trim reinforcing the stress points at the top and bottom. True to the staff's proud assurances, the four-pronged fork seemed sharp, maybe even too much for the elementary school students who typically used these tools (this assessment informed by my 15 years of school administration with "safety first" forming the key guiding principle). The staff explained that safety protocols are part of the curriculum, and students do have to demonstrate correct handling of the tools. While we were in the garden, they used a kitchen example: Students use real knives in the kitchen and are trained on proper technique, including holding the food with one hand as a claw, the fingers folded under at the knuckle to lessen the risk of extremities being accidentally cut, and making short movements with the knife. They also stressed safe care of the tool itself, with the knife being placed blade-side facing away from the chef at the top of the cutting board when not in use, a practice I have since adopted in my own kitchen at home.

With our pitchforks, Josh and I moved to the morning's first task. Spring planting was in process, and we were to help. After a quick demonstration from the staff, we set about using the pitchforks to turn over chunks of dirt from a slightly raised bed about 3-feet across and maybe 30-feet long. Once the bed was generally loosened, we went back over it, spearing the bigger dirt clods with the fork to further break them apart. The goal was to create a smooth, loose, and slightly raised bed. We achieved the goal. The combination of physical movement, the fresh air, and the warming sun also resulted in our jackets being tossed aside.

Having prepared the bed, we moved on to planting. The seedlings had been planted in the greenhouse. The staff explained that the greenhouse provided a better environment for planting seeds, before moving the seedlings to the outdoor garden beds that we were preparing. The edible schoolyard we were in is very well developed. Indeed, the staff affectionately refers to it as the "mothership." This garden was the first in what has become a network of edible schoolyards with accompanying kitchens, spanning the region and including the urban, suburban, and rural elementary schools at the focus of this study. The gardens are not limited to PK-12 schools. Gardens are also implemented at both the local university and community college, where they provide opportunities for agricultural education, socio-emotional learning with connectedness to others and to the earth that so many students crave in this screen-driven post-pandemic age, and fresh produce for students available through the schools' food pantries. As the original location, this garden forms the model for other gardens and kitchens. The curriculum is developed here. New processes are experimented with here, which is symbolized by the greenhouse. The greenhouse was recently completed and built using grant money from supporters, including local businesses in the agricultural and healthcare industries interested in furthering edible schoolyard education. In other words, the sophisticated garden we were experiencing this spring morning did not appear all at once but emerged a little at a time, starting small, like a seed, and growing into the fruit-bearing field apparent today.

We planted our lettuce seedlings, each one about three inches high. We staggered the plantings, allowing enough room for each plant to grow into its full-sized mature form. Standing back, we admired our work while brushing dirt off our hands. Our hands got dirty again as we laid flexible brown piping along the length of the bed to provide the young plants with irrigation. The staff appeared with arches made of curved pieces of white PVC pipes, about three feet across and maybe a foot high. We placed these arches every few feet along the bed's length and covered them with black netting. The staff provided instructions regarding folding the excess netting into a neat roll along the length of the bed and using a little metal stake to firmly pin the netting to the ground. Apparently, birds love these vegetables just as much as we do, and the netting helps ensure there will be a harvest in a few months. While we felt bad for the hungry birds, we did learn that the presence of other organisms that want this food is a sign of an appropriate and functioning ecology. If nothing wants to eat what is growing, you probably shouldn't eat it either!

Finishing with the seedling bed, we pruned the brightly colored red, yellow, and green rainbow chard beds. The chard was mature and needed its smaller shoots which were growing under a foot-and-a-half, or so, to be plucked off by hand to allow more air and light among the plants. While some of the plucked pieces could be used for salads in the kitchen, most of today's pruning was destined to be consumed by different hungry organisms. We moved the wheelbarrow full of chard over to the raised worm bed. Made of lumber readily available from a local big-box construction supply store, the worm bed sat about waist high and was a rectangle of about 4 feet by 6 feet and a foot deep. Its hinged plywood lid was easily lifted to reveal several inches of rich dirt-like compost. A cockroach ran away from the light, but again, the bug seemed neither out of place nor gross in this decomposition area. The area's ecology seemed to be working.

Digging through the dirt revealed earthworms. Rainbow chard prunings were thickly laid on top, and we are sure the earthworms were pleased with their new meal. While the worms perform an important function in contributing to compost creation, they will also be released into the garden to continue their essential work.

Our morning ended with a stop at a much larger compost pile. We added the remaining chard prunings to other plant prunings in various stages of decomposition. As a then-hungry human being, I imagined the nutritious and delicious lettuces, chards, carrots, grapes, potatoes, and strawberries (to name a few) the compost would contribute to as the ecological circle of life continued. As a teacher, I imagined the possibilities of connecting these life cycle and ecology insights to classroom lessons as experiential learning. The literal dirt on the students' hands provided tangible connections to the readings, diagrams, lectures, discussions, and projects that could grow out of these authentic and engaging garden experiences.

The Philosophic Roots

While the engaging and arguably authentic experiences we had in the garden that bright spring morning seem novel and even exceptional for modern American education, the philosophic roots actually extend quite deep. Over a century ago, John Dewey (1915/2010) surveyed the early 20th-century educational landscape dominated by rote chalk-and-talk learning that offered little personal meaning for students, and suggested that "only by being true to the full growth of all the individuals who make it up, can society by any chance be true to itself" (p. 5). Harkening to the modern call to build a more irresistibly-just world (Benjamin, 2022), Dewey proposed a new vision of authentic and meaningful educational experiences for students that critiqued and challenged the standardized curriculum of his day. This tension still exists today as educators work to meet the accountability mandates of rote standardized testing, often at the expense of meaningful and authentic experiences that holistically build academic knowledge, a sense of self-worth, and active citizenship within a community (Apple, 2018; Dewey 1938/2007, 1915/2010, 1916/2016; Ylimaki, 2011). In essence, the choice then is the same as the choice now, between standardized learning leading to a controlled and standardized society or experiential learning leading to individual capabilities for functioning in a democratic community.

For Dewey (1915/2010), the school garden provided one means of creating the authentic, engaging, and democratic education he envisioned. The school garden was not merely a place to grow flowers or vegetables but a laboratory where teachers and students alike experienced more academic concepts. Even in today's era of the Common Core-based standardized testing environment, a growing movement of creating and tending school gardens (Ozer, 2007) has been shown to increase student motivation and engagement (Skinner et al., 2012; Passy, 2014; Ruiz-Gallardo et al., 2013) while increasing learning in science (Wells et al., 2015), health and nutrition (Hazzard, 2011; Robinson-O'Brien et al., 2009), and physical activity (Rees-Punia et al., 2017).

On a professional level, Dewey's words regarding engaging, authentic experiences as the goal of learning ring true. I started my educational career in the fall of 1995 in an urban—back then we called it inner-city—high school in the Tucson, Arizona area. I taught freshman World History and was fortunate enough to be part of a team of teachers with whom I collaboratively planned what we hoped were engaging and authentic experiences. The team included an English teacher, a science teacher, and a physical education teacher. We shared the same 120 students across the same four-hour time block. So, we could teach each class separately for an hour at a time following the normal bell schedule, or we could creatively arrange our time, such as teaching all 120 students together across the shared four-hour time block. In practice, we used the shared time for activities, including a Greco-Roman civilization festival where students wore toga costumes (school-appropriate) and brought Greek and Roman food for a shared potluck. The festival included student presentations of classical drama scenes, readings of their poetry, and Lincoln-Douglas-style debates on topics such as the role of the Olympics in society. All the activities in this culminating event were drawn from a month-long unit featuring lessons across the four academic disciplines.

Content competency was important, but so were the processes involved. While the role of the Olympics might be an interesting topic, formulating research and fact-based positions, presenting those positions, and responding to questions rationally are processes essential to a functioning democracy regardless of one's view about the Olympics. The critical thinking involved arguably forms a foundational skill much more valuable than any student's view of the Olympics themselves.

While our school's Greco-Roman festival stands out in my memory as a particularly engaging and authentic experience, there were others across the year, including campus community service activities, a hike featuring geologic and biologic sciences in a nearby state park, and a community-building event utilizing the high school's pool.

Missing from these fond memories is any requirement to meet or exceed any standards. As a professional learning community, we happily created our own curriculum, instruction, and assessments, building in the activities we hoped would engage and inspire students over the better half of a decade. Only towards the end did the administration come to us to talk about state standards while providing some vague and somewhat ominous hints about required testing soon to come. Whereas before we could exercise our own professional creativity, now we increasingly invested valuable time and energy into creating curriculum maps and connecting specific activities with specific standards. Creativity became less about what we believed was best for students and increasingly about what was best to meet requirements imposed upon us by the state and the school. With standardized testing looming, we began to question whether the activities we cherished were worth the time and energy. Would our instructional efforts pay dividends on the state test results, or should we focus on drilling the knowledge and skills we expected to be on the test? In other words, were we free to pursue a Deweyesque version of education, or were we constrained by what was expected on a rote test? The forces of drill, skill, and rote learning that Dewey challenged a hundred years ago still dominate our educational landscape and shape our common sense regarding what education might, or should, be.

We faced this decision in the early 2000s, about a generation ago. As a nation, we have now experienced over 20 years of No Child Left Behind (NCLB) and the Common Core. An entire generation has completed formal schooling without knowing a world without standardized testing. Demonstrating competence in reading, writing, and mathematics, as demonstrated on a common test, is not in and of itself a bad thing. Indeed, these basic skills form the foundation of success in a functioning and free society. The challenge arises from the overly extensive emphasis on the Partnership for Assessment of Readiness for College and Careers (PARCC) and Smarter Balanced tests as what is valued; in addition, how the value is measured is limited. Nevertheless, educators including teachers, principals, and superintendents know that their job performance and how positively the community perceives their schools rests on these results. Choices have to be made regarding how instructional time is utilized, with priority often given to packaged and purchased programs promising test results and usually backed by some large-scale, data-based marketing campaigns. Teachers become mere curriculum implementers to produce results determined by others. Indeed, not only do our students not know a world without testing and the accompanying school grades prominently displayed in the media and on state-provided dashboards, but increasing numbers of teachers have never experienced a world without standardization. Our capacity to educate for student-centered, authentic, engaging, and ultimately meaningful education for a functioning, free, and democratic society is waning.

This challenge has not gone unnoticed. Writing for the *Academy Book Series in Education*, Boyles (2020) addresses the critical question of what education might be by drawing from Dewey in promoting an imaginative vision of teaching, characterized by inquiry and committed to diverse student interests addressing social problems. In the same series but in a different book, Mallory and Davis (2019) emphasize building an invitational school culture characterized by love, while Rose (2019) continues to emphasize that students do not love schools that do not love them back. They emphasize the need to move away from the cold rigor of standardized testing, a sentiment reiterated by Zhao's (2019) examination of how test-driven education in China forms a manual for how to make children hate school. The same lessons apply to the United States, with McCardle et al. (2019) emphasizing that standardized testing has created an experience for children that is disturbingly different from their own classroom experiences, contributing to distrust and even hatred of schooling and driving the growing opt-out movement where parents refuse to let their children take the standardized tests.

Opting out of the standardized testing regime does form one critique of today's educational environment. The opt-out movement emphasizes parental rights and community control rather than corporate or increasingly distant state and federal mandates over parents and their children (Lingard & Hursh, 2019; Szolowicz, 2020, 2021). However, while the opt-out movement does provide a powerful critique of and resistance to the standardized testing regime, it falls short in two important areas.

First, standardized testing enjoys broad bi-partisan support. The first nationwide testing mandate was imposed nationally by a bi-partisan vote of Congress during Republican George W. Bush's presidency. Further emphasizing the broad bi-partisan support for standardized testing, Democratic President Barack Obama reinforced standardized testing through his Race to the Top initiative and the subsequent state adoptions of the more rigorous standards in the Common Core. Subsequently, the federal government, along with states and schools, have poured millions into the creation of accompanying PARCC and Smarter Balanced-based tests, created public webpages such as California's dashboard to publicize testing results, and invested in test preparation strategies. Considering the substantial investment and bi-partisan support, standardized testing shows few signs of going away soon.

Second, and perhaps more importantly, while opt-out challenges what is, the movement offers little in terms of what could, and even should, be. This work addresses the need for a viable educational vision based on authenticity and student engagement while recognizing that such a vision faces steep challenges in the current policy environment. In this sense, the battle that Dewey started over 100 years ago remains to be fought. In fact, during the research leading to this book, one of the four study schools intentionally reduced the time its students were spending in the garden and kitchen, choosing instead to approach the testing challenge with more drill. Still, there may be room for steps toward such a student- and community-based vision that move the country forward and result in a better way of education. I suggest, as did Dewey, that gardens and their accompanying kitchens where students can grow, prepare, and eat their food provides a pathway for education that is more meaningful to students, emphasizing real-world problems and solutions, while also providing authentic rather than test-prep opportunities for students to connect with the commonly accepted reading, writing, and mathematics requirements assessed on standardized testing.

The Growing Plant

This book grows in two stages. First, Chapters 2 through 4 explore the theoretical foundations of garden and kitchen education. Chapter 2 addresses the theoretical foundations of engaging education in an age of standardization. The chapter addresses key concepts from Dewey, offers insights into how Dewey and others applied these insights, and discusses critical curriculum leadership, which draws from Dewey to discuss the role of engaging and student-centered learning in an age of standardized testing. Chapter 3 furthers the theoretical groundwork by examining self-determination theory (SDT). SDT supports Dewey by examining the roles of purely intrinsic forms of motivation versus externalized motivators. SDT has been applied in multiple educational, business, and community settings, including previous work regarding school gardens, and focuses on the roles of competence, autonomy, and relatedness. In our study schools, we present student survey results related to SDT's competence, autonomy, and relatedness. Chapter 4 begins by exploring previous school garden and kitchen literature and ends with a description of the schools involved in this case study (Yin, 2018).

All the schools involved in this study feature acre-sized school gardens, have accompanying kitchens where students prepare food, and are supported in part by the efforts of a local educational foundation dedicated to gardening and kitchens. The foundation provides financial support, develops project and curriculum ideas, experiments with new gardening and kitchen concepts, and provides professional development for garden and kitchen instructors. The schools cover a range of demographics, including urban, suburban, and rural. Two schools are part of a charter school network specifically formed to incorporate edible schoolyards into the school experience. The other two are regular public schools committed to the edible schoolyard experiment.

The second growth stage focuses more closely on our study schools in Chapters 1 through 9. These chapters draw primarily from 25 semi-structured interviews with garden educators, kitchen educators, program specialists, activity leaders, classroom teachers, special education teachers, assistant principals, principals, a charter school network CEO, and an educational foundation president. Seven participants have their children enrolled in the study schools, thus providing a parental perspective. True to a grounded qualitative research approach (Corbin & Strauss, 2015), we seek to provide rich descriptions of the participants' experiences and perspectives, using their own words as much as possible. While the participants' experiences form the fertile foundation, we also draw upon our participation in garden and kitchen work, observation of lessons and professional development, and related social media.

The chapters in this second stage progress as follows: Chapter 5 examines each role's leadership in forming and sustaining a school culture grounded in edible schoolyards. Chapter 6 examines the educators' favorite projects for learning and provides insights and suggestions into how to utilize garden and kitchen resources for learning. Chapter 7 builds on this theme by discussing connections between garden and kitchen learning and learning in the classroom. Implications for standardized testing, both potentialities and limitations, are shared. While the participants in the study schools currently enjoy the fruits of well-developed gardens and kitchens reflecting years of financial, time, and energy investments, many had also been around at the beginning. Chapter 8 suggests ideas and resources for starting an edible schoolyard experience. We conclude in Chapter 9 with a reiteration of why edible schoolyard and kitchen learning experiences are important today as examples of student-centered, engaging, and authentic education.

The tension between rote standardized learning and learning based on student-centered, engaging, and authentic real-world experiences continues as it has for the 100-plus years since Dewey laid out a vision for more democratic education. What we think about and do with the forms of education that challenge the standardized testing status quo create key critical questions about the legacy we create for our children and the future of our democratic society.

References

Apple, M. W. (2018). *The struggle for democracy in education: Lessons from social realities*. Routledge.

Benjamin, R. (2022). *Viral justice: How we grow the world we want*. Princeton University Press.

Boyles, D. (2020). *John Dewey's imaginative vision of teaching: Combining theory and practice*. Meyers Education Press.

Corbin, J., & Strauss, A. (2015). *Basics of qualitative research: Techniques and procedures for developing grounded theory* (4th ed.). SAGE Publications, Inc.

Dewey, J. (2007). *Experience and education*. Simon and Schuster. (Original work published 1938).

Dewey, J. (2010). *The school and society and the child and the curriculum* (2nd ed.). Digireads.com publishing. (Original work published 1915).

Dewey, J. (2016). *Democracy and education*. Ozymandias Press. (Original work published 1916).

Hazzard, E. L. (2011). *Utilization of garden-based education to positively impact children's nutrition knowledge and behaviors*. [Unpublished doctoral dissertation]. University of California, Davis.

Lingard, B., & Hursh, D. (2019). Grassroots democracy in New York State: Opting out and resisting the corporate reform agenda in schooling. In S. Riddle & M. W. Apple (Eds.), *Re-imagining education for democracy* (pp. 238–255). Routledge.

Mallory, B. J., & Davis, J. (2019). Invitational learning: Building school culture with love. In S. P. Jones & E.C. Sheffield (Eds.), *Why kids love (and hate) school: Reflections on practice* (pp. 16–33). Myers Education Press.

McCardle, T., Currin, E., & Schroeder, S. (2019). From the pickup line to the picket line: Opt out's love-hate relationship with public schools. In S.P. Jones & E.C. Sheffield (Eds.), *Why kids love (and hate) school: Reflections on practice* (pp. 178–192). Myers Education Press.

Ozer, E. J. (2007). The effects of school gardens on students and schools: Conceptualization and considerations for maximizing healthy development. *Health Education & Behavior, 34*(6), 846–863. https://doi.org/10.1177/1090198106289002

Passy, R. (2014). School gardens: Teaching and learning outside the front door. *International Journal of Primary, Elementary, and Early Years Education, 42*(1), 22–38. https://doi.org/10.1080/03004279.2011.636371

Rees-Punia, E., Holloway, A., Knauft, D., & Schmidt, M. D. (2017). Effects of school gardening lessons on elementary school children's physical activity and sedentary time. *Journal of Physical Activity and Health, 14*, 959–964. https://doi.org/10.1123/jpah.2016-0725

Robinson-O'Brien, R., Story, M., & Heim, S. (2009). Impact of garden-based youth nutrition intervention programs: A review. *Journal of the American Dietetic Association, 109*(2), 273–280. https://doi.org/10.1016/j.jada.2008.10.051

Rose, B. J. (2019). Beyond curriculum: Students don't love school when schools don't love them back. In S.P. Jones & E.C. Sheffield (Eds.), *Why kids love (and hate) school: Reflections on practice* (pp. 34–52). Myers Education Press.

Ruiz-Gallardo, J. R., Verde, A., & Valdés, A. (2013). Garden-based learning: An experience with "at risk" secondary education students. *The Journal of Environmental Education, 44*(4), 252–270. https://doi.org/10.1080/00958964.2013.786669

Skinner, E. A., Chi, U., & The Learning-Gardens Educational Assessment Group. (2012). Intrinsic motivation and engagement as "active ingredients" in garden-based education: Examining models and measures derived from Self-Determination Theory. *The Journal of Environmental Education, 43*(1), 16–36. https://doi.org/10.1080/00958964.2011.596856

Szolowicz, M. A. (2020). Opposing versus supporting opting out of standardized testing: Policy subjectivity in the state legislative process. *The SoJo Journal: Educational Foundations and Social Justice Education, 6*(1–2), 97–112.

Szolowicz, M. A. (2021). Disassembling efforts to legalize opting-out in Arizona: A case study of legislative politics. *Teachers College Record, 123*(5), 1–22. https://doi.org/10.1177/016146812112300511

Wells, N. M., Myers, B. M., Todd, L. E., Barale, K., Gaolach, B., Ferenz, G., Aitken, M., Henderson, C. R. Jr., Tse, C., Pattison, K. O., Taylor, C., Connerly, L., Carson, J. B., Gensemer, A. Z., Franz, N. K., & Falk, E. (2015). The effects of school gardens on children's science knowledge: A randomized controlled trial of low-income elementary schools. *International Journal of Science Education, 37*(17), 2858–2878. https://doi.org/10.1080/09500693.2015.1112048

Yin, R. K. (2018). *Case study research and applications: Designs and methods* (6th ed.). SAGE Publications, Inc.

Ylimaki, R. (2011). *Critical curriculum leadership. A framework for progressive education.* Routledge.

Zhao, L. (2019). A manual on how to make children hate school: The case of test-driven Chinese education. In S. P. Jones & E. C. Sheffield (Eds.), *Why kids love (and hate) school: Reflections on practice* (pp. 125–135). Myers Education Press.

CHAPTER TWO

ENGAGING EDUCATION IN AN AGE OF STANDARDIZATION

As an undergraduate student in a teacher education program, I had professors who repeatedly talked about how important and influential the American educational philosopher John Dewey is to education. John Dewey is an American philosopher and educational reformer who wrote extensively with, "over 50 books, approximately 750 articles, and countless addresses, reviews, and encyclopedia entries," attempting to address what he saw as false dualisms in American life and particularly education (Fishman & McCarthy, 1998, p. 15). These dualisms, or mutually exclusive choices, included the choices between authoritarianism and democracy on a broad scale, and rote learning and student-centered or socially-based learning on a more specifically applied scale. Dewey lived and worked around the turn of the last century, with his most famous works including *The School and Society and The Child and the Curriculum* (Dewey, 1915/2010) and *Democracy and Education* (1916/2016) being published over a century ago. Despite Dewey's importance to education, though, I was never assigned to read any of Dewey's work as part of my preparation program. This emphasis on Dewey's importance, yet no formal discussion of his work, was repeated through my subsequent master's and doctoral degrees. Further, I was not alone in this experience. While finally engaging in reading Dewey in preparation for this project on edible schoolyards, I was pleasantly surprised to find a former mentor, Dr. Gary Fenstermacher (2006), also recollecting his own experiences with rediscovering Dewey. As he re-opened his copy of *Democracy and Education* purchased decades earlier, he found a note he had written, saying that he bought the book because he "felt I should have it" (Fenstermacher,

2006, p. 109). Dr. Fenstermacher revisited the book only to prepare to write a chapter he was writing, much as I began my exploration of Dewey in earnest only when asked to do so at a Critical Questions in Education conference in relation to starting this book project.

I suspect Dr. Fenstermacher's and my mutual approach to Dewey, paying homage to and recognizing his importance without exploring what that might be, is not entirely unusual in education. Even a professor working at the University of Chicago, where Dewey himself thought and taught, and focusing on Dewey as a core of her classes, admits to not reading Dewey's *Democracy and Education* until called upon to contribute a book chapter (Feiman-Nemser, 2006). H.M Kliebard, who had read, analyzed, and utilized Dewey as part of his study regarding how the American curriculum was forged (Kliebard, 1992), acknowledges the broad consensus of Dewey's influence but then argues that Dewey's actual influence is quite negligible (Kliebard, 2006). Kliebard makes a point that "many of [Dewey's] ideas on the curriculum run contrary not only to conventional practice but to what many of the leading reformers in the curriculum world tried to promote" (Kliebard, 2006, p. 114).

Dewey emphasized growth and captured the first dualism in the opening chapter of *The School and Society* (1915/2010); he suggests that we typically look at school from an individualistic perspective where what interests us most naturally is the progress made by the individual child in their ability to, "read, write, and figure, his growth in the knowledge of geography and history, improvement in manners, habits of promptness, and industry—it is from these standards that we judge the work of the school" (pp. 3–4). So far, Dewey's acknowledgment of what we conventionally look for in a school does not sound that different from what we experience today. Standardized testing, for example, emphasizes the individual's ability to demonstrate their reading, writing, and math abilities on a standardized test. We still use the collective impressions of the students' reading, writing, and math abilities to judge our schools' effectiveness. The key difference between today and 100 years ago when Dewey was writing is that the focus is not on the content of *what* we emphasize but perhaps on the extent of *how* we view it. In Dewey's day, education focused on classrooms with students sitting in straight rows, silently reading from common readers, and sometimes some students responding to questions asked by the teacher, usually standing up front. While this image of education could easily be found in many classrooms around the country today, in Dewey's day, that vision of education existed largely because an alternative had not been proposed. In other words, there was no alternative view of what education could or should be. Today, thanks to Dewey's work, which we will explore in more depth shortly, there is an alternative view. Still, that alternative, progressive view of education remains an insurgent alternative view, struggling against the common paradigm as a result of the emphasis placed on testing, with its accompanying accountability measures publicly displayed through news media and state school dashboards measuring each school's performance in a competitive marketplace (e.g., Apple, 2005, 2014, 2018, 2019; Hursh, 2007, 2016; Watkins, 2012; Ylimaki, 2011, 2012). When Kliebard (2006) writes that the goals of educational reformers run contrary to Dewey's vision, this is what he means; as modern reformers, at least in the last 20 years since No Child Left Behind, have largely reinforced the rote learning Dewey sought to change. That the idea of placing a garden or a kitchen in a school seems radical or even simply out of place testifies to the power our standardized assumptions of education hold.

Dewey (1915/2010) addresses the other side of the dualism, starting with the individual, by discussing a social view of education; he writes, "What the best and wisest parent wants for their own child, that must be what the community wants for all its children. Any other ideal for our schools is narrow and unlovely; acted upon, it destroys our democracy" (p. 5). In emphasizing the importance of the love a parent has for their child, the hope for success and advancement that arises from that love, and implying the role schools play in fulfilling that hope, Dewey introduces a social aspect of education. Education is not merely for the individual, and not merely for the individual to perform better than their peers in the market-based competition of a neoliberal society, but rather for the individual operating within the cooperative relationships of a social society, the social society starting with familial relationships. While I write, "rather," Dewey (1915/2010) actually sees individualism and this social view of education as one: "Only by being true to the full growth of individuals who make it up, can society by any chance be true to itself" (p. 5). Dewey concludes that any discussions of any new movements in education must take into account the broader social view, lest the reforms seem like just another passing fad.

Two important points emerge from the above paragraph, democracy and growth, and yet both are intimately connected in Dewey's view. Let's focus first on the broader concept of democracy. Hansen (2006) suggests that democracy, to Dewey, was something richer and more generative than an electoral process and system of political structures. In Hansen's view, democracy to Dewey was a much deeper concept than what political party one voted for or even the act of voting and engaging in representative politics itself. Instead, democracy is another name for a social, rather than purely individualistic, approach to life and education. In this social approach to life, democracy becomes a synonym for inquiring, communicating, and learning. Note that inquiring implies a degree of agency on the student's part that extends beyond the rote memorization of facts provided by the teacher while sitting still and quietly in neatly arranged rows. Such a regulated system, it would seem, is more appropriately suited to a system of control rather than one that develops the innate interests and talents of the individual student. Dewey (1916/2016) addresses this in *Democracy and Education*, where he compares the coercive force used to create a bond of a union based on the simple capacity to fear. In other words, fear, such as the fear of public humiliation from low test scores, precludes free engagement in play or authentic activities relevant to life among social group members. Dewey proceeds to suggest that a diversity of stimulations, or experiences, provides novelty which provokes challenging thoughts. The more challenges to thought, the less routine, rote, or capricious is the learning, leading to higher agency whereby students can engage in activity that is socially serviceable, develop a personal interest, and foster freedom to question in whose service they are engaged.

Fenstermacher (2006) explores the tension between fear and freedom, which can also be expressed as state control and student agency, more thoroughly by suggesting that any diminution of the students' agency by systems of control diminishes human flourishing and weakens democracy. Fenstermacher (2006) suggests that agency includes the "freedom and capacity of the student to actively engage his or her intelligence" (p. 102). Note the emphasis on action and engagement on the student's part. This active engagement of intelligence is key to the formation of democratic living as Dewey (1916/2011) defined democracy:

> A democracy is more than a form of government; it is primarily a mode of associated living, a conjoint communicated experience. The extension in space of the number of individuals who participate in an interest so that each has to refer his own action to that of others, and to consider the action of others to give point and direction to his own, is equivalent to breaking down those

> barriers of class, race, and national territory which kept men from perceiving the full import of their activities. (p. 66)

That democracy, to Dewey, is more an organic way of life and less a formal system of government is clear. That organic way of life depends on everyone's participation, implying agency and engagement while considering the impact of their actions on the well-being of the whole. If this is democracy, the methods by which children gain their education in their formative years will either promote or hinder their future ability to participate in an effective democratic society. Indeed, schooling itself, in its methods and opportunities for students to actively engage their intelligence within the social bonds of a group, will either promote or hinder a democratic society.

As Knoll (2022) emphasizes, the child and the child's interactions with their environment were to be the starting point of education. Subject matter, reading, writing, math, history, and geography are important but are to flow from the agency the child exhibits through meaningful interactions in quality experiences. As Dewey (1916/2011) stated:

> The instinctively mobile and eagerly varying action of childhood, the love of new stimuli and new developments, too easily passes into a "settling down," which means aversion to change and a resting on past achievements. Only an environment which secures full use of intelligence in the process of forming habits can counteract this tendency. (p. 38)

It is through these interactions that growth occurs. But growth toward what ends? Again, the social view is critically important, as subjects should not be taught for their own ends and isolated from everyday life but instead are legitimized by their relation to real life. Knoll (2022) suggests This legitimization takes the form of three key growth areas:

1. Natural development – strengthening the student's innate powers and resources;

2. Social efficiency – enabling the student's participation in social and economic life; and

3. Individual culture – the student's attaining useful community knowledge and ethical values.

Notice how two of the three growth objectives, social efficiency and individual culture, clearly involve socialization, the student's relationships with others in their community, businesses, and broader society. The remaining objective, natural development, focuses on the individual but finds meaning as the habits formed in development find full expression, not in individual use but in use in conjunction with and in service to others.

In fact, this social interaction, the ability to understand, work within, and even influence the environment, forms the heart of Dewey's (1916/2011) definition of education as expressed in *Democracy and Education*:

> Education is not infrequently defined as consisting in the acquisition of those habits that effect an adjustment of an individual and his environment. The definition expresses an essential phase of growth. But it is essential that adjustment be understood in its active sense of control of means for achieving ends. If we think of a habit simply as a change wrought in the organism, ignoring the fact that this change consists in ability to effect subsequent changes in the environment, we shall be led to think of "adjustment" as a conformity to environment as wax conforms to the seal which impresses it. (p. 35)

Again, the emphasis is on action in acquiring habits, that is, growth, and then in further growth by using those acquired habits to effect change in their personal, social, and cultural environments. Habits provide an increase in ease, economy, and efficiency for action. These action-oriented habits mark an intellectual disposition of an active preference and choice for conditions that allow the habit to be exercised. Change-effecting habits assume the individual's familiarity with the materials and equipment to which the action is applied. Habits include observation and reflection leading to the development of skills that make one "an engineer, an architect, a physician, or a merchant. In unskilled forms of labor, the intellectual factors are at a minimum precisely because the habits involved are not high grade;" high-grade habits, Dewey continues, include judging and reasoning "as truly as handling a tool, painting a picture, or conducting an experiment" (Dewey, 1916/2011, p. 37). Again, these are action-oriented and require active engagement with and within the student's social and physical environment. Such active engagement far exceeds what is possible in the controlled and relatively sterile classroom environment.

The pursuit of how to best develop the habits for effective interactions in a functional democracy raises another of Dewey's dualisms. As stated by Dewey, "There is, accordingly, a marked difference between the education which every one gets from living with others, as long as he really lives instead of just continuing to subsist, and the deliberate educating of the young" (1916/2011, p. 4). Here, Dewey reiterates the importance of education's primary objective: to build social relationships, through the emphasis on "living with others." The dualism emerges from differing means by which children, "the young," develop this social capability. All children, or the "every one" Dewey mentions, are naturally educated through their relationships with their caretakers, that is, the "living with others" necessary in early life. Dewey proceeds to explain that this informal means of education is "incidental, natural, and important" (1916/2011 p. 5). Implicit in the "incidental" nature of the informal educative experiences is the critique that each informal experience varies in quality regarding the experience's potential for preparing children for future social interactions in societal institutions, including economic, domestic, political, religious, and legal settings.

Dewey (1916/2011) explains, "As civilization advances, the gap between the capacities of the young and the concerns of the adults widens. Learning by direct sharing in the pursuits of grown-ups becomes increasingly difficult except in the case of the less advanced occupations" (p. 6). Informal education in a complex society such as ours is insufficient for the adequate preparation of children for future social interactions. Here, the second part of this dualism emerges as informal education must be supplemented and supported by formal education, which is the point of schools. Dewey reiterates the importance of formal education's primary goal: "Since our chief business with them is to enable them to share in a common life we cannot help considering whether or not we are forming the powers to secure this ability" (p. 5). Dewey explains that while childhood play that imitates adult occupations is a sufficient education, it is only to a point, as much of what adults do is remote in both space (away from home and school) and meaning. Much of adult social interaction in an advanced and complicated civilization such as ours is embedded in symbols—that is, through the written page. As such, the:

> Ability to share effectively in adult activities thus depends upon a prior training given with this end in view. Intentional agencies—schools—and explicit

> material—studies—are devised. The task of teaching certain things is delegated to a special group of persons.
>
> Without such formal education, it is not possible to transmit all the resources and achievements of a complex society. It also opens a way to a kind of experience which would not be accessible to the young, if they were left to pick up their training in informal association with others, since books and symbols are mastered. (Dewey, 1916/2011, p. 6)

Formal education, including emphasis on training in the written word through which so much of the experiences of modern society are contained, must therefore supplement the informal education of childhood play.

What this formal education entails is the subject of much discussion, starting with Dewey himself (e.g., Dewey 1938/2007; 1915/2010, 1916/2016; Dewey & Dewey, 1915/1962) and extending to countless works over the last century (e.g., Boyles, 2020; Kliebard, 2006; Knoll, 2022; Page, 2006). In essence, the dualism of how to best apply Dewey's theory to practical use in real classrooms might be best expressed as another synonymous dualism, asking to what extent should the child direct their own education (informal education based in play) versus to what extent should teachers in schools direct the child's education (formal education based in written symbols or reading). Dewey, himself, while recognizing and promoting at least some degree of formal education, admits, "There is the standing danger that the material of formal instruction will be merely the subject matter of the schools, isolated from the subject matter of life experience" (Dewey, 1916/2011, p. 7), and even more bluntly, "Formal instruction, on the contrary, easily becomes remote and dead—abstract and bookish, to use the ordinary words of depreciation" (p. 6). Later in *Schools of Tomorrow*, Dewey and Dewey (1915/1962) contrast natural student growth with this bookish and dead style of teaching, describing the latter as putting "a premium upon accumulating information in the form of symbols. Quantity rather than quality of knowledge is emphasized; results that may be exhibited when asked for rather than personal attitude and method," (p. 10). One needs only to look at the drill and skill test preps to which so many students are subjected, not to mention the tests themselves, to appreciate the prescience of Dewey's warning.

On the one hand, then, deadening bookishness is best avoided. On the other hand, there is another extreme of allowing the student too much freedom, which also does not adequately capture Dewey's vision. In other words, who controls the curriculum, the student or the teacher, in formal educative schooling? Knoll (2022) addresses the issue of student freedom versus teacher guidance first by acknowledging that Dewey strongly supported children being expressive and realizing their authentic selves. In Knoll's (2022) view, Dewey's emphasis on "self-activity," "self-expression," and "self-realization" was "basic" to Dewey's vision (p. 47). However, as the agent of formal education, the teacher has an important role in utilizing the student's self-expression to make it function as an instrument in bringing the child to a new consciousness, that is, new learning. The teacher, therefore, fills an important role in facilitating or guiding the instruction. In this, the teacher does have to perform a delicate "balancing act" in paying attention to the interests of the individual child, but also "to take into account the impulses and interests shared by all children so that group instruction would be ensured, and social skills could be developed and strengthened" (Knoll, 2022, p. 49). In this balancing act, the teacher still controls the curriculum but does so in a way that recognizes individual interests and social needs. The teacher is neither irrelevant nor a sage on the stage, but rather a guide on the side, working to avoid the "tragic error," of being, "so anxious for results that we neglect the process of growing" (Dewey & Dewey, 1915/1962, pp. 4-5).

In practice, what does facilitating the process of growing look like? Dewey and Dewey explore this notion in some practical detail in *Schools of Tomorrow* (1915/1962), where they hope to suggest the practical meaning of some of their more widely recognized views of educational reform. In their own words, the teachers and schools presented demonstrate the desired tendencies toward greater freedom, the identification of the child's school life with the environment, and the recognition of education's role in a democracy. Their schools represent urban and rural schools, the suburbs being a social development that does not really occur until a few decades later, after World War II. Two major themes emerge from the vignettes presented. First, there is an emphasis on the health, well-being, and growth of the whole child, not just an emphasis on learning what might be considered academic content such as reading, writing, and arithmetic. Second, there is an emphasis on age-appropriate experiential learning to supplement and even supplant book learning.

The Dewey's (1915/1962) visit to Mrs. Johnson's classroom in Greenwich, Connecticut begins with a sharp critique of the typical schoolroom:

> Nature has not adapted the young animal to the narrow desk, the crowded curriculum, the silent absorption of complicated facts. His very life and growth depend on motion, yet the school forces him into a cramped position for hours at a time, so that the teacher may be sure he is listening or studying books. (p. 15)

Rather, time is intentionally built into the school day for movement and motion:

> The child with the well-nourished, active body is the child who is most anxious to do and to know things. The need of the activity must be met in the exercise of the school, hour by hour; the child must be allowed to move about both in work and in play, to imitate and to discover for himself. The world of objects around him is an unexplored hemisphere to the child even at the age of six years, a world constantly enlarging his small vision as his activities carry him further and further in his investigations. (Dewey & Dewey, 1915/1962, p. 15)

While the above example's emphasis is on young children, one can visualize the child exploring a rich and stimulating but set and defined area, and the implications for future growth are obvious. As the child grows, so do the parameters of the objects for exploration within the environment. One might start the exploration of the outdoors, for example, in a small school garden and continue it in local parks and even nearby wilderness. Regardless of the environment explored, the keys here include the provision of movement, exercise of both body and mind within the environment, and the opportunity for the child to engage in inquiry.

Books are still used in Mrs. Johnson's school, and reading is still important, but the method is different from the typical classroom of the era (and arguably, many of today):

> At Fairhope, the children do the work and the teacher is there to help them know, not to have them give back what they have memorized. Tests are often conducted with books open, since they are not to show the teacher what the child can remember, but rather to discover his progress in the ability to use books. Lessons are not assigned, but the books are open in the hands of the pupil and with the teacher they discuss the text, getting out of it all the joy and information possible. (Dewey & Dewey, 1915/1962, p. 21)

The spirit of inquiry already suggested by the active interactions with the environment further permeates the interactions with the book learning. Books here are not used in a deadening process of memorization but rather are used openly and inquisitively to further understand and explore the child's world.

The two major themes, the whole child and experiential learning, can be seen in what the Deweys and Mrs. Johnson call "field geography:"

> The children go into the fields and woods and look at the trees and flowers, ask questions about them, examine the differences in bark, leaves, and flowers, tell each other what they think, and use their books to answer questions that the trees and plants have suggested to them. They learn the meaning of the words pistils, stamens, and petals with flowers they have gathered, or watch a bee carrying pollen from plant to plant. Individual pupils are encouraged to tell the class what they have learned at home, to bring flowers from their gardens, or to tell of things they have seen. (Dewey & Dewey, 1915/1962, p. 24)

The movement of children through the fields and woods provides the basis for physical and mental growth. Physical growth occurs as the students walk and otherwise exercise, while mental growth occurs as they observe, discover, and question their environment. Through the exercise, students seek to answer their questions and, in the process, learn typical academic-type concepts, in this case, the naming of the parts of the flower. True to Dewey's vision, the activity is not merely individualistic, although individuals will ask and answer their questions, but also social in orientation. Here, students "tell the class" insights from their own learning, their own homes, and their own observations.

The relationships in experiential learning are further explored through the experiments conducted in Public School 45 in Indianapolis, Indiana. Here, the Deweys explicitly address the connections between student-driven experiential learning and potentially deadening book learning by explaining:

> Learning by doing does not, of course, mean the substitution of manual occupations or handwork for textbook studying. At the same time, allowing pupils to do handwork whenever there is an opportunity for it is a great aid in holding the child's attention and interest. (Dewey & Dewey, 1915/1962, p. 54)

The experiences of Public School 45 (PS 45) help clarify the balance, or dualism, of book and experiential learning and add another wrinkle. Specifically, PS 45 attempted to use the methods of learning by doing while simultaneously addressing the requirements of the state curriculum. Here, the teachers are "constantly finding new ways to prevent the work becoming a mere drill in textbook facts, or preparation for examinations" (Dewey & Dewey, 1915/1962, p. 54). A variety of learning experiences are presented, including a fifth-grade class's creation of plans for a bungalow and expanding the plans to place the house on a farm they designed; a study of the purpose and workings of the Panama Canal that had students exploring geopolitical relations through an imagined war between Japan and the United States (keep in mind World War II was still about 25 years in the future from when *Schools of Tomorrow* was first published); a third-grade class's set-up of a parcel post system; and a first-grade class's creation of a retail shoe store.

The plans for the farm provide particular insights into the connections between the real world and engaging problem-solving of designing a farm while also addressing reading, writing, math, biology, geography, and other academic topics while doing so:

> The children very soon invented a family for their house and decided they would have them live on a farm. The arithmetic work was then based on the whole farm. First, this was laid out for planting, plans were drawn to scale, and from information the children themselves gathered, they made their problems, basing them on their play farm such as the size of the cornfield, how many bushels of seeds would be needed to plant it; how big a crop they could expect, and how much profit. The children showed great interest and ingenuity in inventing problems containing the particular mathematical process they were learning and which still would fit their farm. They built fences, cement sidewalks, a brick wall, did the marketing for the family, sold butter, milk, and eggs, and took out fire insurance. When they were papering the house the number of area problems connected with buying, cutting, and fitting the paper were enough to give them all the necessary drill in measurement of areas. (Dewey & Dewey, 1915/1962, p. 56)

The students in this fifth-grade class were clearly enjoying the creation of their own world; one can picture a modern classroom using Minecraft or similar build-your-own-universe technology to create an updated version of this turn-of-the-last-century lesson. Yet arithmetic is not neglected, with the finding of area specifically mentioned and the math involved with assessing risk implied through the purchasing of fire insurance. Experience and academics are merged.

The question of balancing or incorporating experiential and academic learning remains relevant today, with possibilities as diverse and creative as teachers and students themselves. Zipin and Brennan (2019) suggest students serve as co-researchers on problems that matter, while others take a similar student-focused and project-based approach in arts education (Thomson et al., 2019). Bellingham et al. (2019) explore educational consciousness focused on community-building efforts in Footscray, Australia to create a pop-up school event that emphasized the community's web of past and present, everyday encounters and relations. Alford et al. (2019) explore the relationship between student experiences and standardized curriculum in Australian and Swedish contexts, drawing extensively from personal and professional (for the teachers) histories. Harris et al. (2019) examine the Children's Voices Project in conjunction with their state's education department to explore how multimodal literacies might be fostered through children's participation in informing state government strategic planning. Smart-Morstad and Triggs (2019) explore children's use of textiles, woodshop, and drama as part of the curriculum at Hateigsskoli in Iceland. Ylimaki (2012) explores, among other examples, Mrs. Minor's English class's work in responding to a community need, such as the soil lead content around the school neighborhood. As the economy in their northeastern United States city declined, older houses with lead paint were abandoned and eventually torn down, resulting in lead contamination of the soil and affecting plants, presumably including local gardens. The students read their textbooks, city reports, and other resources, using what they learned to create their own reports which they presented to a parent group and the city council. One parent was "astounded at the quality of the children's work. Their papers were well written, grammatically correct, and informative" while making "passionate and professional" presentations (Ylimaki, 2012, p. 31).

Ylimaki's (2011, 2012) work bears particular interest for this project in three ways. First, Ylimaki's (2012) work is firmly based on Dewey's progressive vision for education:

> [A] democratic way of life is not a means to some larger end or outcome. It is in itself the realization of political, social, and educational ends supportive of

> growth. According to Dewey, such a democratic society must have a type of education that gives individuals a personal interest in social relationships and control, and the habits of mind that secure social change without introducing disorder. (pp. 308-309)

Second, Ylimaki explores the role that community-based, project-centered, en- gaging, authentic learning might play in a new era of standardized testing. While state curriculum standards marked Dewey's time, the introduction of No Child Left Behind in 2001, about a century after Dewey's writings, added a new national requirement for standardized testing to measure how effectively schools were teaching and students were learning the basics of reading, writing, and math. This new accountability mechanism placed new pressures on educators, including teachers and principals, to successfully meet the new demands. Third, Ylimaki's work focuses on the role of leadership within this new reform era. While Ylimaki (2011) implicitly recognizes distributed leadership's role (e.g., Hallinger, 2003; Harris et al., 2007; Leithwood & Jantzi, 2005) among teachers, principals, and other educators, she primarily focuses on the transformative potential of principal leadership.

In the age of standardized testing, Ylimaki identifies two significant leadership approaches to the challenge of achieving standardized testing success: new professional curriculum leadership and critical curriculum leadership. The new professional principals' first leadership pathway responds to the demands of external standardized accountability by shifting their schools' emphases toward skills-based instruction that promises quick improvements in student academic achievement. The new professional principals, over time, become increasingly reliant on textbooks and externally developed "research-based" models of instruction. The new professional principals manifest a no-nonsense approach to curriculum, focusing on standards, pre-packaged curriculum, and tests rather than students' and their communities' cultural backgrounds and social issues. These principals develop strong reputations as experts in the management of externality, and perhaps because of these reputations, develop a sort of disdain for the leadership displayed by the critical curriculum leadership shown by other principals.

In this second leadership pathway, critical curriculum developers make conscious decisions to engage their students in community-based curriculum development processes emphasizing equity among white students, students of color, and students living in poverty. These critical curriculum leaders lead community-based curriculum efforts in which teachers, parents, and students identify goals and social change projects that inspire community revitalization, student agency, growth, and empowerment. Like their new professional colleagues, the critical curriculum leaders also emphasize academic achievement and see their efforts result in rising student academic achievement as reflected on standardized measures.

However, in a crucial difference, the critical curriculum leaders see the standardized achievement results as a byproduct of the more authentic, engaging, project-based, or service learning their school communities develop rather than the end goal in and of itself. Nevertheless, despite the academic and social achievements of these critical curriculum leaders, their new professional colleagues still look at them with a sort of haughty disdain, as expressed by one new professional's statement, "[Peer Principal] spends way too much time on service-learning projects. It's fine to plant flowers, but let's plant the basic skills first" (Ylimaki, 2012, p. 327).

Planting flowers, which conjures up related gardening imagery, is a historically apropos means of distinguishing the key differences and resultant tensions between student engagement and authentically-driven schooling versus rote and standardized schooling. John Dewey (1938/2007; 1915/2010) set the stage for these divergent philosophic streams of education over a century ago, in part by suggesting a school garden as the model or essence of an authentic, engaging, child-centered education for democracy:

> I wish to suggest that really the only way to unite parts of the system is to unite each to life. . . . This block (A) in the center represents the school system as a whole. (1) At one side we have the home, and the two arrows represent the free interplay of influences, materials, and ideas between the home life and that of the school. (2) Below we have the relation to the natural environment, the great field of geography in the widest sense. The school building has about it a natural environment. It ought to be a garden, and the children from the garden would be led on to surrounding fields, and then into the wider country with all its facts and forces. (3) Above is represented business life, and the necessity for free play between school and the needs and forces of industry. (Dewey, 1915/2010, p. 44)

Note that Dewey emphasizes the central role of nature and growth in a child's education in this brief example, much to the disdain of new professional educators a century later, if not to his contemporaries. Yet, Dewey also recognizes the interrelatedness of the garden to the school and the home and even business to the school. Dewey's education was not only about planting flowers but planting flowers to promote the child's growth and support active citizenship in the family, community, and business. Boyles (2020) interprets Dewey's imaginative vision through the lens of pragmatic instrumentalism—that is, that the child's educative experiences should have transformative consequences as they engage in everyday behavior and activity.

In suggesting school gardens as a critical feature of formal schooling, Dewey is providing suggestions on how to address the central problem of experience-based education—that is, what kind of experiences might be selected to provide both a lively encounter for students and creatively promise future fruitful experiences (Dewey, 1938/2007). Dewey repeatedly mentioned, explored, and explained the importance of garden and kitchen education as a practical means to implement his vision (Dewey 1915/2010, 1916/2016, 1938/2007; Dewey & Dewey, 1915/1962). In *Experience and Education*, Dewey (1938/2007) justifies kitchens, shops, and similar experiences:

> not just [because] they afford opportunity for activity, but [because] they provide opportunity for the *kind* or for the acquisition of mechanical skills which leads students to attend to the relation of means and ends, and then to consideration of the way things interact with one another to produce definite effects. It is the same in principle as the ground for laboratories in scientific research. (p. 84)

In other words, gardens and kitchens in experiential education should be more than places where students grow pretty flowers. They should also operate as laboratories for inquisitive exploration with the habits of mind, including means and ends and interactions within the system studied, understood, and applied.

Dewey (1915/2010) explores the mechanics of garden and kitchen education in much more depth in *The School and Society and The Child and the Curriculum*, and the exploration is worth quoting in depth:

> That the dining-room and the kitchen connect with the country and its processes and products it is hardly necessary to say. Cooking may be so taught that it has no connection with country life, and with the sciences that find

> their unity in geography. Perhaps it generally has been taught without these connections being really made. But all the materials that come into the kitchen have their origin in the country; they come from the soil, are nurtured through the influence of light and water, and represent a great variety of local environments. Through this connection, extending from the garden into the larger world, the child has his most natural introduction to the study of the sciences. Where did these things grow? What was necessary to their growth? What's their relation to the soil? What's the effect of different climatic conditions? And so on. We all know what the old-fashioned botany was: partly collecting flowers that were pretty, pressing and mounting them; partly pulling these flowers to pieces and giving technical names to the different parts, finding all the different leaves, naming all their different shapes and forms. It was a study of plants without any reference to the soil, or to growth. In contrast, a real study of plants takes them in their natural environment and in the uses as well, not simply as food, but in all their adaptations to the social life of man. Cooking becomes as well a most natural introduction to the study of chemistry, giving the child here also something which he can at once bring to bear upon his daily experience. (Dewey, 1915/2010, pp. 50–51)

Dewey's garden and kitchen education vision extends far beyond growing pretty flowers. To provide authentic experiences that promote habits of mind for effective democratic living, the resources of gardens and kitchens need intentional links to broader academic subjects such as botany and chemistry. The teacher's role is strongly implied in the preceding vignette as the guide who observes the child's exploration of their environment, notices their questions and interests, and guides the child through effective questioning toward broader academic concepts. The teacher and other school leaders, including the principal, bear responsibility for providing the garden and kitchen facilities, allowing student exploration within these facilities, and guiding the connections to further content and the habits of gaining knowledge, understanding, application, analysis, synthesis, evaluation, and creativity essential to the individual's capacity to create and sustain life in a democratic society.

References

Alford, J., Schmidt, C., & Lyngfelt, A. (2019). Critical literacy as legitimate knowledge: The importance of teacher agency. In S. Riddle & M. W. Apple (Eds.), *Re-imagining education for democracy* (pp. 91–110). Routledge.

Apple, M. W. (2005). Doing things the 'right' way: Legitimating educational inequalities in conservative times. *Educational Review, 57*(3), 271–293. https://doi.org/10.1080/00131910500149002

Apple, M. W. (2014). *Official knowledge: Democratic education in a conservative age* (3rd ed.). Routledge.

Apple, M. W. (2018). *The struggle for democracy in education: Lessons from social realities.* Routledge.

Apple, M. W. (2019). *Ideology and curriculum* (4th ed.). Routledge.

Bellingham, R., Thomas, M. K. E., Charman, K., Dixon, M, & Cooper, J. (2019). What is valued knowledge and where does it live? In S. Riddle & M. W. Apple (Eds.), *Re-imagining education for democracy* (pp. 74–91). Routledge.

Boyles, D. (2020). *John Dewey's imaginative vision of teaching: Combining theory and practice.* Meyers Education Press.

Dewey, J. (2007). *Experience and education.* Simon and Schuster. (Original work published 1938).

Dewey, J. (2010). *The school and society and the child and the curriculum* (2nd ed.). Digireads.com publishing. (Original work published 1915).

Dewey, J. (2011) *Democracy and education.* Digireads.com Publishing. (Original work published in 1916).

Dewey, J. (2016). *Democracy and education.* Ozymandias Press. (Original work published 1916).

Dewey, J., & Dewey, E. (1962). *Schools of tomorrow.* E. P. Dutton & Co., Inc. (Original work published 1915).

Feiman-Nemser, S. (2006). A teacher educator looks at *Democracy and Education.* In D. T. Hansen (Ed.), *John Dewey and our educational prospect: A critical engagement with Dewey's Democracy and Education* (pp. 129–145). State University of New York Press, Albany.

Fenstermacher, G. D. (2006). Rediscovering the student in *Democracy and Education.* In D. T. Hansen (Ed.), *John Dewey and our educational prospect: A critical engagement with Dewey's Democracy and Education* (pp. 97–112). State University of New York Press, Albany.

Fishman, S. M., & McCarthy, L. (1998). *John Dewey and the challenge of classroom practice.* Teachers College Press.

Hallinger, P. (2003). Leading educational change: Reflections on the practice of instructional and transformational leadership. *Cambridge Journal of Education, 33*(3), 329–351. https://doi.org/10.1080/0305764032000122005

Hansen, D. T. (2006). Preface. In D. T. Hansen (Ed.), *John Dewey and our educational prospect: A critical engagement with Dewey's Democracy and Education* (pp. vii–ix). State University of New York Press, Albany.

Harris, A., Leithwood, K., Day, C., Sammons, P., & Hopkins, D. (2007). Distributed leadership and organizational change: Reviewing the evidence. *Journal of Educational Change, 8*, 337–347. https://doi.org/10.1007/s10833-007-9048-4

Harris, P., Peterson, A., & Brock, C. (2019). Re-imagining young children's literacy education for their democratic participation. In S. Riddle & M. W. Apple (Eds.), *Re-imagining education for democracy* (pp. 111–126). Routledge.

Hursh, D. W. (2007). Assessing No Child Left Behind and the rise of neoliberal education policies. *American Educational Research Journal, 44*(3), 493–518. https://doi.org/10.3102/000283 1207306764

Hursh, D. W. (2016). *The end of public schools: The corporate reform agenda to privatize education*. Routledge.

Kliebard, H. M. (1992). *Forging the American curriculum: Essays in curriculum history and theory*. Routledge.

Kliebard, H. M. (2006). Dewey's reconstruction of the curriculum: From occupation to disciplined knowledge. In D. T. Hansen (Ed.), *John Dewey and our educational prospect: A critical engagement with Dewey's Democracy and Education* (pp. 113–127). State University of New York Press, Albany.

Knoll, M. (2022). *Beyond rhetoric: New perspectives on John Dewey's pedagogy*. Peter Lang Group AG, International Academic Publishers.

Leithwood, K., & Jantzi, D. (2005). A review of transformational school leadership research 1996–2005. *Leadership and Policy in Schools, 4*, 177–199. https://doi.org/10.1080/1570076 0500244769

Page, R. N. (2006). Curriculum matters. In D.T. Hansen (Ed.), *John Dewey and our educational prospect: A critical engagement with Dewey's Democracy and Education* (pp. 39–65). State University of New York Press, Albany.

Smart-Morstad, K., & Triggs, S. (2019) Icelandic education at Hateigsskoli: Giving students wings. In S. P. Jones & E. C. Sheffield (Eds.), *Why kids love (and hate) school: Reflections on practice* (pp. 125–135). Myers Education Press.

Thomson, P., Hall, C., Earl, L., & Geppert, C. (2019). Towards an arts education for cultural citizenship. In S. Riddle & M. W. Apple (Eds.), *Re-imagining education for democracy* (pp. 173–189). Routledge.

Watkins, W. H. (2012). The new social order: An educator looks at economics, politics, and race. In W. H. Watkins (Ed.), *The assault on public education; Confronting the politics of corporate school reform* (pp. 7–32). Teachers College Press.

Ylimaki, R. (2011). *Critical curriculum leadership: A framework for progressive education*. Routledge.

Ylimaki, R. M. (2012). Curriculum leadership in a conservative era. *Educational Administration Quarterly, 48*(2), 304–346. https://doi.org/10.1177/0013161X11427393

Zipin, L., & Brennan, M. (2019). Pursuing pragmatic-radical curriculum democracy: Students as co-researchers on problems that matter. In S. Riddle & M. W. Apple (Eds.), *Re-imagining education for democracy* (pp. 55–72). Routledge.

CHAPTER THREE

EDIBLE SCHOOLYARDS YESTERDAY AND TODAY

SCHOOL GARDENS HAVE RATHER deep roots in American education, as suggested by Dewey, who wrote over 100 years ago at the turn of the 20th century. The plants that compose gardens have a natural life cycle. Indeed, as will be explored in a later chapter, observing, interacting, explaining, and applying this lifecycle of seed, seedling, plant, harvest, and decay to create the nutrient-rich compost needed to sustain the next generation forms a favorite lesson of edible schoolyard educators. Likewise, gardens themselves follow a lifecycle often tied to planting, tending, harvesting, and restoration seasons in preparation for the next planting season. The natural rhythms of the garden further suggest the cycles of school reform in the century from Dewey's time to ours. Desmond et al. (2002) suggest three significant waves of garden education, each creating and challenging the prevailing norms of its time:

- the early 20th century (1900-1930) – Progressive Education and Social Reform movements encourage garden-based learning,
- the mid-20th century (1960-1970) – Counterculture and Environmental movements create a resurgence in school gardens,
- the late 20th century (1990-2000) – Rebirth of Progressive Education coupled with renewed interest in environmental education and nutrition/health issues for children (p. 16).

In addition to these three eras of garden education, our own time, roughly 2015 to the present, forms another season of garden education that builds upon the rebirth of Progressive Education and seeks alternatives to standardized testing, which has now dominated American education for a generation.

Dewey, of course, was both a major initiator and philosopher of the Progressive era of educational and social reform of the early 20th century, 1900 to 1930, and emphasized themes such as learning by doing, problem-solving, and the social skills and sense of community responsibility necessary for a thriving democratic society. The Progressive educator's main challenge was, and remains, the tension between this child-centered yet holistic approach to education and those who see schools as fundamentally teacher-centered, authoritative academic spaces where children should learn the basics of reading, writing, math, and little else (Tenuto, 2014). Progressive educators at the turn of the 20th century established gardens in a wide range of schools, including urban and rural settings, regular public schools, and specialized schools such as Dewey's own experimental Laboratory School (Kohlstedt, 2008).

In addition to the Deweyan progressive philosophy of education, turn of the 20th-century garden proponents were motivated by a variety of practical factors. One was the desire for agricultural education as promoted by the United States Department of Agriculture, a move that was in part influenced by the growing urbanization and industrialization of American life, leading to a related fear that the essential skills and knowledge needed for life-sustaining food would be lost as people adapted to new lives working in factories and living in cities (Kohlstead, 2008; Trelstad, 1997). Another came during World War I with the rise of "victory gardens" as President Woodrow Wilson called upon Americans, and the nation responded by creating backyard, community, and school gardens to plant vegetables, thus freeing valuable food commodities to feed the soldiers overseas. The federal government promoted the civic virtues of wartime school gardens through the "Join the United States School Garden Army" campaign and was further supported through youth organizations such as the Boy Scouts' "Every Scout to Feed a Soldier" movement (Kohlstead, 2008; Trelstad, 1997; Wake, 2015). The Boy Scouts, along with the Girl Scouts, also formed summer camps, which further influenced back-to-nature study in a wilderness setting that complemented the garden movement; this was in line with Dewey's suggestion that the child should move from the immediate local community, such as the garden, to broader nature studies. The Scouting movement also played a role, along with the schools, in promoting gardens and in addressing the new wave of immigration occurring during the Progressive Era.

In addition to urbanization and industrialization, the Progressive Era saw one of the largest periods of mass immigration to the United States. This was the era of Ellis Island through which millions of mostly eastern and southern European immigrants arrived in the United States, sailing past the newly built Statue of Liberty. School gardens were seen as a means for providing experiences familiar to many immigrants arriving from European farms and being familiar with Europe's rich history of school gardening (Atchoarena & Gasperini, 2004; Jagiello et al., 2021) that drew from both historical philosophers, including Rousseau and Froebel and contemporary thinkers such as Dewey and Montessori. By 1905, there were over 100,000 school gardens across Europe (Desmond et al., 2002). Based on their inherent interest in building local community and a strong democracy, Dewey and the Progressives also grappled with the challenges of integrating newly arrived immigrants into schools, specifically, and American society, generally. The need was great. Between 1900 and 1915, New York City schools alone doubled in size, by adding 400,000 students, due in part to immigration and in part to new child labor laws requiring children to attend school rather than work in the factories (Trelstad, 1997). The Deweys share their observation of immigrant parents interacting with a school garden in Chicago:

> The advantage to the school was great, for a large group of foreign parents came into close touch with it, discovered that it was a real force in the neighborhood, and that they could cooperate with it. This element of the population usually stands quite aloof from the school its children go to, through timidity and ignorance, or simply through feeling the institution is above them. (Dewey & Dewey, 1915/1962, pp. 70–71)

Here the Deweys emphasizes the welcoming and even democratizing function of the school garden for those who might see the school itself as something foreign and unwelcoming. The garden becomes a vehicle for community-building, as reported by Trelstad (1997, where the DeWitt Clinton School Farm in New York City created "a bright spot out of an admittedly bleak neighborhood" (p. 165) and attracted over 1,000 children from the nearby immigrant neighborhoods. Trelstad further reports that many school gardens followed DeWitt Clinton's example and built gardens in vacant lots near immigrant communities with several objectives, including beautifying the city, teaching the value of manual labor, and Americanizing the children. Because the gardens largely grew vegetables rather than flowers, they further served economic and public health goals.

Yet the attempt to "Americanize" immigrant children might also contain the seeds of why school gardens fell out of favor, or to use gardening terms, went dormant in the 1930s. Trelstad (1997) and Wake (2015) suggest several factors explaining the decline of school gardens, starting with a philosophical argument. Neo-Marxist critiques of Progressive educational reform argued that as gardens were used to promote the value of manual labor and as economic vehicles for harvesting vegetables, they became less community-building mechanisms and more means for imposing traditional social control mechanisms, preparing strong, healthy children for future labor. In other words, some viewed social control and class dominance as the garden's true purpose. However, other societal factors were also at play. The invention of the automobile led to the creation of the first suburbs and a move from school gardens to home gardens, permitted by the larger backyards of suburban living. A decline in the capacity of teachers to provide instruction in growing agricultural products also contributed. While many teachers could grow individual plants, they increasingly lost the knowledge of how to grow crops as a profession. Teachers also found it easier to change care-intensive gardens to grass, which was far simpler to grow and maintain. This shift coincided with a societal shift from gardens to beautify urban landscapes to parks. Schools increasingly adopted the philosophy of parks by creating playgrounds featuring grass fields. Urbanization and industrialization contributed to the school garden's decline as it became increasingly apparent that training future farmers was not as much of a priority as it had been with advances in agriculture technology and the availability of factory jobs. Expressed simply, cities provided a means to earn a living that did not require farming ability. Finally, immigration quotas ended the period of mass immigration symbolized by Ellis Island and the Statue of Liberty, thus reducing the number of immigrant students in schools and the related need for socialization or Americanization.

The early Progressive Era of the early 1900s was marked by considerable amounts of societal change, as urbanization saw people moving from farms to cities; industrialization saw people working in factories according to the rhythms of mass production regulated by a clock rather than the seasons and daylight; and mass immigration changed the ethnic, religious, and cultural identity of America. The era also saw the first systematic emergence of school gardens in the United States. It is perhaps then fitting that the second spring for American garden education also occurred during a time of immense societal upheaval and change, the 1960s and 70s (Desmond et al., 2002; Moore, 1995). Education during this time was deeply affected by world events, particularly the Soviet Union's launch of the first artificial satellite to orbit Earth, Sputnik, in October 1957. The launch of Sputnik within the context of the Cold War between the Soviet Union and the United States sparked alarm and even panic and fear in the latter. Americans watched the satellite passing overhead, some listened to its beeping through the radio, and wondered what other surprises, especially nuclear surprises, the Soviets might produce next. The United States reacted with a renewed national emphasis on winning the space race both in peaceful scientific exploration, such as landing on the moon, and in closing the "missile gap," whereby it was believed the Soviet Union possessed far more nuclear-armed missiles than did the United States. Both the peaceful and military fronts in the space race placed a new emphasis on math, science, and technology to train the new generation of future scientists and engineers who would maintain American technological prowess. In the immediate aftermath of Sputnik's launch, for example, Congress passed the National Defense Education Act of 1958 which provided funding for students majoring in math and science, boosted college and university enrollment across the country, and was justified as a national security necessity.

With the emphasis on space and technology, perhaps even because of this emphasis, some began to wonder why more was not being done to take care of the planet already inhabited. Famously during this time, the Cayahuga River in Cleveland, Ohio caught fire 14 times, most notably on June 22, 1969, as a result of pollution from industrial waste. Years earlier, Rachel Carson (1962) sounded an environmental alarm when she published *Silent Spring*, addressing issues of environmental harm from indiscriminate pesticide use. Images of the earth taken from astronauts on and orbiting the moon showed a tiny planet in the vastness of space, a perspective never really seen before. These images and events spurred political reforms such as the creation of the Environmental Protection Agency by President Nixon in 1970 and also, arguably, contributed to a renewed interest in fresh healthy food that was not watered by rivers that could catch on fire nor grown in land contaminated with pesticides and who knows what else.

One such garden movement is described by Moore (1995) in recounting the experiences of The Environmental Yard, a project that stretched over a ten-year period starting in the early 1970s. Alarmed at the disconnect between children and their environment, and especially alarmed at television's impact on keeping children passively indoors, Moore (1995) reasoned:

> If sustainable development values are to be created in society, we must recreate, as a matter of great urgency, viable educational habitats for children where they are able to learn on a daily basis the lessons of nature. Gardening is clearly an effective first step. (pp. 223–224)

In describing this project begun in the early 1970s, Moore captures some themes we have already seen in previous gardening efforts from the Progressive Era and expands on others that will continue into present day. First, gardens cannot be produced alone. The Environmental Yard project was a cooperation between the University of California, Berkeley, and the Berkeley School District, both major educational institutions. Collaboration also occurred at a micro-level, with Moore stating, "much of the success of the project stemmed from a close collaboration between the author as an environmental designer/researcher and Dr. Herb Wong, then principal of Washington School" (1995, p. 224). This relationship between design, research, and the schools recreated Dewey's vision of collaboration among many parts of society, including the school, families, and businesses. As the Environmental Yard project grew, local businesses became involved in donating seeds, hand tools, and even truckloads of topsoil.

Yet, while collaboration among community interests played a key role in the garden's development, individual leadership also played a prominent role. The principal, Dr. Herb Wong:

> had a single minded passion to develop interdisciplinary environmental pedagogy at the school. For him, this meant that all subject areas would be taught through the environment because of the strong motivation that all children have to explore their physical surrounding through play and to make their own discoveries. This approach ensures that children also learn about the environment. (Moore, 1995, p. 224)

Leadership—especially strong visionary leadership from the principal, a teacher leader, or community advocate—forms a key theme in successful school garden initiatives. Energetic advocacy requires providing a vision for what the garden can accomplish and then working to make that vision a reality by securing financial support and by motivating teachers to adapt to the new opportunities the garden provides.

In the Environmental Yard project, the principal and his staff of teachers set out to utilize the garden they were building to make direct connections between the classroom and nature, between indoor and outdoor learning. A problem-solving approach was taken as students learned about planting seedlings, providing water by improving the irrigation system, building protection for the tender plants from errant balls from nearby games, and composting. Regarding composting, one class conducted a simple but controlled experiment, authentically utilizing the scientific process in a manner that would make Dewey proud, by planting some beans with compost and others without and then comparing the growth rates. (The composted plants won the growth race.) In another example, a class practiced numeracy skills with recently harvested pumpkins, including measuring and weighing the pumpkins, then subsequently estimating and counting the seeds.

That this project emerged in Berkeley is perhaps not surprising for several reasons. First, as Moore himself points out, the school had already had a garden back in the 1920s, during the Progressive Era. That garden disappeared in the post-World War II era, as asphalt replaced gardening. Second, Berkeley in the 1960s became a hotbed of the American counterculture, symbolized by the hippies, and showed an openness to progressive ideas from the past and for the future. Further, Berkeley was also the home of the restaurant Chez Panisse and its founder, Alice Waters.

When it came to food, perhaps no one better captured the counterculture and environmental ethos of the mid-20th century than Alice Waters. On the website for the modern Edible Schoolyard project (The Edible Schoolyard, 2024), Waters is described modestly as, "a chef, author, food activist, and the founder and owner of Chez Panisse Restaurant in Berkeley, California." Desmond et al. (2002) describe Waters as, "a prominent figure in the school garden and organic cultural movement as well as the founder of 'The Edible Schoolyard' in Berkeley, California" (p. 20). Waters describes herself as having held only two professions in her life, one as a teacher in the Berkeley Montessori School during "a period of enormous social upheaval, so it was an exciting time; every parent and teacher seemed to feel that we could bring about a more just society by working together," and the other as the founder of Chez Panisse (Waters, 2008, p. 5).

While working as a teacher, Waters took a trip to Paris and there discovered a passion for French food and the "way it anchored French family life to an agricultural community and even to the seasons" (Waters, 2008, p. 5). She returned to Berkeley and opened the restaurant named after a character in an old French movie and sought to provide food prepared from fresh, seasonal, delicious ingredients obtained from nearby local farmers, ranchers, and dairymen. She also hoped her friends would join her there for tasty food while talking politics, and especially the right way to bring up children and how to save the planet. Waters' emphasis on fresh local ingredients was countercultural for the time. The technology-driven culture of the 1960s emphasized math and science education, the space race, television, and, in the culinary realm, technological, industrially prepared food. McDonald's and other fast food restaurants were rapidly growing at this time, places where you could drive up in your car and drive away eating a hamburger that would taste the same no matter what the season—fall, winter, spring, or summer. The region did not matter either. The hamburger or whatever processed food, such as frozen TV dinners, would taste the same whether purchased and consumed in California or New York or anywhere in between. The industrially processed consistency was key, and the disconnect from the environment was never considered or questioned. Into this milieu stepped Chez Panisse, inspiring what we would today call the farm-to-table movement emphasizing seasonal, local, organic food that was delicious, nutritious, and that re-connected people with the environment from which their sustenance came.

While Waters is best known for her restaurant and the farm-to-table movement it started, her few years as a Montessori educator also play a key role in her later involvement in the school garden movement. Maria Montessori was a contemporary of Dewey's and, like Dewey, emphasized a child-centered approach to education. While Dewey started a laboratory school to explore how to make connections between academics and the environment, Montessori took child-centeredness to a different level by emphasizing self-directed learning, essentially allowing the child to choose when, what, and even how they would learn. John and Evelyn Dewey (1915/1962) address Montessori's methods in a chapter aptly titled Freedom and Individuality:

> [T]he difference between the Montessori method and the views of American reformers lies not in the difference of opinion as to the value of liberty, but rather in a different conception of the best use to be made of it. Physically, the pupils in a Montessori class are freer than they are in the classes of most American educators with whose views this book has been dealing; intellectually they are not so free. (p. 115)

Practically speaking, the Deweys were concerned that Montessori had too narrow a definition of freedom that allowed for great individuality but did not connect that individuality to greater social good or even to the development of higher cognitive faculties (Knoll, 2022). If a child chose to not socialize, they did not have to socialize. If a child chose not to read, they would not read. Despite differences regarding the extent of a child's freedom versus teacher direction and control in the classroom, Dewey and Montessori still shared an interest in educating the whole child with an emphasis on real-world experiences. School gardens played a major role in both educators' approaches to education, including the garden's emphasis on movement, an appreciation of nature, authentic experiences, and moral development (e.g., Blair, 2009; Desmond et al., 2002; Jagiello et al., 2021; Rahm, 2002). These values were in turn shared by Alice Waters and inspired her return to education.

While Waters opened Chez Panisse in the early 1970s, her interest in school gardens started growing in the mid-1990s. As such, her experience and influence serve as a bridge between the second spring of American garden education and third spring starting in the late 20th century. Waters' experience with starting the Edible Schoolyard at Martin Luther King, Jr. Middle School in Berkeley, California contains now-familiar themes. Like Moore (1995) and the earlier Progressive Reformers, she became concerned about a neglected schoolyard in her neighborhood:

> The city of Berkeley has a great university, but its public schools rank among the poorest in the United States. . . . [T]hat middle school was a rundown collection of sad old concrete buildings with peeling paint and a hard blacktop playground. Countless windows lay broken with no money to fix them, and a few lawns grew long and wild in the rainy season and dried yellow in the summer. Graffiti was commonplace. The school looked so poorly attended, I wondered if it might not be abandoned. (Waters, 2008, p. 7)

Waters continues to describe the school's demographics, including the 1,000 students who were enrolled there and the English as a Second Language program serving immigrant children speaking over 20 different languages. In viewing this decrepit nature of the school facilities, she questioned her own faith in public education, wondering how the children could thrive in such an environment and what message the environment sent about our culture's priorities.

The desire to see students thrive became the key to Waters' schoolyard efforts and the fertile soil of motivation from which her efforts grew. Her visionary leadership included seeing students growing their own healthy food—she specifically mentions heirloom tomatoes and golden raspberries—while learning about science such as biology, ecology, and chemistry. History could be taught through experiences such as the grinding of wheat into flour and the subsequent baking of bread. Importantly, Waters also included a kitchen where students could prepare and eat the food they had grown themselves. In doing so, the students would absorb "almost by osmosis the relationship between the health of our bodies, our communities, and the natural world" (Waters, 2008, p. 10) Echoes of Dewey's emphasis on active learning, connecting the experiences of the natural world and the classroom's academics, and the health of the whole child are clearly heard in Waters' vision.

In implementing her vision, Waters demonstrated the same collaborative leadership as seen in previous gardening efforts such as those undertaken by Moore (1995). Waters published an article in the local newspaper which attracted the attention of the school principal who subsequently approached Waters in the hope of establishing a partnership, thus demonstrating his own visionary and change leadership. Waters (2008) described what she saw on their first walk together:

> The only food the children could buy on campus came from a prefabricated building about the size of a shipping container. Parked in the middle of the asphalt, this building sold soda pop to the children during their recess and lunch hour, and it also sold something called a "walking taco," which is as perfect a symbol of broken culture as I can imagine. Opening a bag of mass-produced corn chips, the food workers would simply pour in a kind of beef-and-tomato slurry from a can. The kids would then walk away, eating on their own with no connection to one another. (p. 11)

While the school district and its superintendent had no money to fix this situation, they also refused to stand in the way of the principal's and Waters' efforts, with the superintendent even volunteering his own time on weekends to help. The growing team faced many of the same challenges previously explored in starting, developing, and maintaining their garden and accompanying kitchen. Labor was needed to clean and clear the abandoned building destined to become a kitchen painted in bright yellow, featuring fresh food posters and colorful flags representing local culture. Tables with red checkered clothes were installed where students could sit together and talk while eating the food they prepared from the artichokes, pumpkins, kale, carrots, spinach, cucumbers, basil, thyme, onions, green beans, and other vegetables they had grown in the acre-sized garden, steps outside the kitchen door. Financial support for these improvements and others such as, needed topsoil and seeds and tools came from building community partnerships. Waters (2008) describes one such partnership where a local farmer "gave us a dozen young olive trees to plant around the perimeter; they've taken root and we've begun to cure our own olives" (p. 38).

Waters' visionary leadership turned an abandoned, inhospitable, unwelcoming, and dysfunctional lot into a thriving farm-to-table school community experience. The combination of the school garden with an accompanying kitchen gave rise to a new term, the "edible schoolyard," reflecting the connection between the two facilities and learning experiences they provide. Her experience with Martin Luther King, Jr. Middle School in Berkeley grew into a larger project, The Edible Schoolyard Project, which captures and likely created the ethos of the late-20th century. Desmond et al. (2002) describe this ethos as a re-birth of Progressive Education, coupled with a renewed interest in environmental education, nutrition, and health issues. The Edible Schoolyard Project prominently and succinctly captures this ethos on their homepage by declaring their pledge to public education as:

- Provide a Free and Sustainable School Lunch for All Students K-12
- Buy Food Directly from Farmers and Ranchers Who Take Care of the Land and Their Workers
- Teach Students the Values of Nourishment, Stewardship, and Community (Edible Schoolyard, 2024)

Started in 1995, The Edible Schoolyard Project remains influential, as seen in Fakharzadeh's (2015) description of edible schoolyards in post-Katrina New Orleans. The Edible Schoolyard Project also serves as the direct inspiration and model for the schools participating in this book's study, right down to the bright yellow paint on the kitchen walls.

This latest season of school gardens and kitchens coincides with significant educational and societal changes just as the first season of Progressive reform coincided with a new era of urbanization, industrialization, and mass immigration; and the second season coincided with a renewed emphasis on math, science, and technology inspired in part by the fears arising from Sputnik and the Cold War's space race between the Soviet Union and the United States. The modern era is also defined by leaps in technology, including the emergence of the Internet. In starting a school garden in the 1970s, Moore (1995) was worried about the impact of television on child development. One must wonder what his thoughts might have been about the impact of today's social media. Moreover, today's educational environment can be seen as a response to increasing globalization (e.g., Dale, 1999; Foster, 2004; Koyama, 2013) wherein nations are increasingly connected through technology such as the Internet and advances in technology such as massive container ships allowing trade among nations at an unprecedented scale. Yet, these connections also bring increased competition among nations and lead to the decline of the local, as jobs previously held in the community can now be outsourced to workers in nations on the other side of the globe. While many goods and services can now be offered much more cheaply, the emphasis on these market-economies, or neo-liberalism, also contributes to increased job insecurity as workers find themselves competing for jobs with others around the world and facing increased economic inequity as wages are driven ever downward by incessant competition.

The neoliberal global economy has led to the reinforcement of the traditional and back-to-basics schooling that Dewey, the Progressives, and many garden and kitchen educators have since resisted. Michael Apple (2005, 2014, 2018) and others (e.g., Ylimaki, 2011, 2012; Szolowicz, 2020, 2021) suggest the current discourse, or what is accepted as common sense in national educational policy, is formed through the uneasy truce among four groups: neoliberals, neoconservatives, authoritarian populists, and new professional managers. As Schirmer and Apple (2016) explain, "Each of these groups prominently embodies one of the key words that have come to define the conservative agenda: markets, standards, God, and inequality" (p. 140). Neoliberalism brings an abiding faith in markets and individual choice, which translates into education by the imposition of competitive norms. In order to inform individual consumers on which schools are the best choices, standards and accompanying standardized tests provide the means to arrive at these choices. Standardized test results publicly reported in newspapers, posted on state dashboards, and spread through social media provide savvy consumers the information needed to inform their choices between "good" and "bad" schools. This selection process is carried out in much the same manner used to choose one car over another based on miles per gallon and projected maintenance costs. But what is to be tested?

The voting power of authoritarian populists who emphasize religious fundamentalism and conservative evangelism must be considered for the neoliberal policies to be implemented. Many populists are also neoconservative in their belief in adherence to traditional moral standards (e.g., the Bible's Ten Commandments) and the accompanying traditional views of schooling. These traditional views emphasize the basics of reading, writing, and mathematics, preferably presented in America's traditional language, English. The new managerial class supports this conservative movement by "providing a swelling class of managers, consultants, and professionals skilled in providing technical tools and justification for both neoliberalism's and neoconservatism's emphasis on accountability, standards, and efficiency" (Schirmer & Apple, 2016, p. 140). Principals, superintendents, and other educational leaders, well aware of the pressure to make the school look good based on test scores, often turn to the new professional class's educational management companies, educational evaluators, and program auditors who provide research-based programs promising to raise test scores. The pressure for educational leaders to take the proven route of more packaged curricula addressing the narrowly defined standardized curriculum and restricting children rather than the counterintuitive route of experiential learning is immense (Williams & Dixon, 2013). The choice to commit valuable school resources including limited funding, limited classroom hours, and limited teacher energy to gardens and kitchens rather than test-prep programs can be considered as boldly countercultural today as it was in Dewey's day.

And yet, many educators do make this choice to provide experiential learning for their students. Blair (2009) notes that 57% of school principals in California indicated that they had instructional gardens or plantings.

Stewart et al. (2013) examines school gardens in the technologies' heartland, California's Silicon Valley. Skinner et al. (2012) discuss school gardens in Portland, Oregon. Fakharzadeh (2015) explores gardens in New Orleans, Louisiana. Kipfer (2018) discusses the implementation, sustainability, and benefits of school gardens in Washington, D.C. Jagiello et al. (2021) explore school garden design in the United States including Manhattan, New York, and Chicago, Illinois, while also explaining school gardens internationally including Stockholm, Sweden; Irkutsk, Russia; Bien Hoa, Vietnam; and Shanghai, China. Dyg and Wistoft (2016) explore student well-being through gardens in Denmark. Huys et al. (2017) also examine implementation practices of school gardens in Denmark. Indeed, the global interest in school gardens is enough that the Food and Agricultural Organization of the United Nations (2004) has offered a common definition of what actually constitutes a school garden: "cultivated areas around or near to primary and/or secondary schools, which can be used mainly for learning purposes but could also generate food and income for the school" (p. 4). The United Nations even offers a manual in their Promoting Lifelong Healthy Eating Habits series, providing teachers, parents, and communities directions for *Setting Up and Running a School Garden* (Food, 2005).

School gardens have become more and more prevalent as a feature of the modern school facility (Ozer, 2007). Many reasons justify this growth. Often mentioned are the gardens' promise for supporting academic performance—especially in the sciences, teaching ecologically sustainable behaviors, teaching knowledge of nutrition and healthy eating, and supporting positive youth development (Skinner et al., 2012). The United Nations expands this list to include academic skills, personal development, social development, moral development, vocational and/or subsistence skills, and life skills (Atchoarena & Gasperini, 2004). Canaris (1995) and Waters (2008) both mention the promotion of healthy eating habits, with Canaris specifically noting that students might clamor for foods they previously did not like. Learning to like new and nutritious foods is also offered as a motivator by Jagiello et al. (2021), who note that fast food has led to a change in eating habits and the fattening of youth. Jagiello et al. further describe socio-psychological effects, as gardens allow students a place to take a breath and relax while facing difficult academics—a challenge itself supported by gardens, especially in promoting learning in sciences.

Therefore, educators in the modern era expect much from their school gardens, kitchens, and the combination of both encompassed by the term edible schoolyard. Essentially, today's expectations can be grouped into two major categories: academics and well-being, with research that addresses both. Starting with academics, Williams and Dixon (2013) comprehensively reviewed school gardens' impact on academic outcomes from 1990 to 2010, with fairly positive results for the school gardening movement. They found that 83% of the 40 reviewed studies promising to assess direct learning outcomes did indeed find positive effects from student experiences in school gardens. Only one of the studies found a negative effect, while 15% suggested learning was unchanged whether students learned through garden experiences or not. Williams and Dixon (2013) continue to provide an encouraging breakdown of garden studies by academic subject area, finding that:

- 93% of studies addressing learning in science showed a positive learning effect (n=15);
- 80% of studies addressing learning math showed a positive learning effect (n=10);
- 72% of studies in language arts showed a positive learning effect (n=11); and
- 67% of studies in writing showed a positive learning effect (n=3). (p. 220)

Social studies were also positively connected to garden learning, with a technical 100% positive learning effect; however, only one study was reviewed in this subject area. Still, Williams and Dixon (2013) were confident enough in the meta-analysis of garden-based learning to conclude that experiences in school gardens "indicate strong and frequently positive impacts in all areas studied" (p. 225). Continuing the meta-analysis methodology, Monferrer et al. (2022) also found studies that suggest experiential garden learning has a positive impact on general academic performance, learning in mathematics, attitudes toward learning mathematics, and both attitudes and learning in other science, technology, engineering, and math (STEM) subjects. However, they did caution that they were not able to establish a direct connection between improved attitudes toward learning and actual learning results.

The findings of these meta-analyses were surely good news for the thousands of school principals in California surveyed by Graham et al. (2005), who reported their perceptions that school gardens were effective in teaching subject matter including science, environmental studies, nutrition, language arts, math, and agricultural studies. Further exploring perceptions, but focusing on students rather than principals, Duncan et al. (2016) found positive student perceptions based on survey data in an urban school. Notably, their findings suggest urban youth, at least at the school in the study, appreciated the experiential learning in both the garden and the kitchen and even preferred the learning experiences provided in the kitchen.

While improving student perceptions of their academic abilities and performance is a valuable goal, confident and engaged students are more likely to continue their education than frustrated and bored students; several studies purport the impact of gardening experiences on actual test scores. Most recently, Davis et al. (2023) set out to explore the connection between gardening experiences provided through the Texas Sprouts program, a gardening, nutrition, and cooking program, and student standardized testing scores. Sixteen schools were involved, with half the schools receiving an intervention in the form of 18 one-hour gardening, nutrition, and cooking lessons, and the other half of the schools receiving no intervention. All schools had a predominantly Hispanic student population and a majority on free and reduced lunch. Study results showed a 6.5 percentage point increase in fourth-grade reading scores on the State of Texas Assessments of Academic Readiness for those schools with gardens over those without. However, no difference was found for fifth-grade reading, and no difference was found in math for either grade. Ray et al. (2016) also compared test scores of schools with and without garden-based learning, this time in Washington, D.C.. They first mapped D.C. schools, with and without gardens, and related community demographics, especially for Black students. Then, using publicly available testing data, they compared schools with and without gardens and found that schools with gardens outperformed schools without gardens in:

- math (56% proficiency in schools with gardens versus 36% proficiency in schools without);
- reading (61% proficiency in schools with gardens versus 38% proficiency in schools without); and

- science (47% proficiency in schools with gardens versus 21% proficiency in schools without).

They conclude, "A central part of our analysis was determining whether there is a significant and positive association between the presence of school gardens in schools and test scores. For math, reading, and science test scores, we found positive support for this proposition," and they further noted that for reading and science scores, this positive association, "persists even when controlling for the race and class composition of the students" (Ray et al., 2016, p. 392). Further, while dated back to just before the start of the No Child Left Behind standardized testing era, Glenn (2000) also found positive evidence of school gardens—positive impact on test scores, such as 100% of third-grade students attending schools with gardens in Milwaukee passing the Wisconsin Reading Comprehension Test compared to a 25% passing rate for students without gardens (p. 5).

Overall, the quantitative research regarding the connections between edible schoolyards and academic results "support[s] the idea that for some students, gardening may be an effective tool to supplement, enhance, or complement existing traditional curricula" (Williams & Dixon, 2013, p. 226). Similarly, research focusing on the well-being of students based on their garden and kitchen experiences also finds encouraging results. For example, Dyg and Wistoft (2016) explore students' experiences in school gardens through multiple case studies in Denmark. Danish gardens are a bit different from those in United States, as the gardens are usually located on farms and other locales off school grounds. Findings still suggest positive impacts on students' positive emotions (e.g., joy, happiness, satisfaction), interpersonal well-being (e.g., connections with other students, relations with nature), self-esteem (e.g., positive self-concept, perceived competence), and behavior (e.g., expressions of empathy, cooperation, civility).

Ratcliffe et al. (2011) focused on a specific measure of well-being and student vegetable consumption, finding that "hands-on garden-based learning experiences can increase low-income urban middle school-aged students' ability to identify vegetables correctly, increase the variety they eat, and increase their consumption of different vegetable varieties at school" (p. 41). Huys et al. (2017) had different findings regarding vegetable consumption in several case study schools they examined. They found no change in vegetable consumption, but they did note that knowledge of vegetables increased through garden work, children's attitudes toward vegetables changed as they were more willing to try vegetables they had grown themselves, and children's overall perception of gardening experiences was positive.

More meta-analyses of the well-being effects of school gardens and kitchens reveal additional positive outcomes. Blair (2009) recognized the re-emergence of school gardening over the previous two decades and identified multiple themes regarding well-being that ran through qualitative studies including:

- students were highly motivated by gardening opportunities to get dirty and explore;
- students showed improved pride in the garden and in the school;
- school gardens promoted strong community-building and teamwork; and
- school gardens provided a diversity of environmental stewardship opportunities.

Likewise, Ohly et al. (2016) expressed similar findings regarding well-being including reducing student stress, building relationships, gaining confidence and self-esteem, and developing teamwork. They also noted multiple studies indicating that gardening contributes to cultural awareness. Parents from non-English speaking backgrounds often felt comfortable in the garden, even if they did not participate in other school activities. The combination of gardening and cooking activities also "provide an opportunity for children to learn about each other's cultures," presumably from growing different vegetables and then preparing them with different recipes (Ohly et al., 2016, p. 30). When provided an opportunity to eat the food they grew and prepared together, the resultant dining experience provided a venue for students to develop and practice their English skills in relaxed and engaged conversations. In this manner, gardens and kitchens can prove beneficial by providing opportunities for mastery and empowerment for students who do not excel in traditional academic settings (Ohly et al., 2016; Williams & Dixon, 2013).

Research, philosophy, and historical experience alike suggest school gardens, kitchens, and the combined efforts seen in edible schoolyards serve as a promising educational model. Here, students engage in authentic, engaging activities that promote growth in academics and well-being. To build upon this rich and fruitful history, we now turn our attention to the edible schoolyards that compose our study.

The four study schools all feature a one-acre sized school garden and an accompanying dedicated kitchen facility. The kitchen facility is specifically designed for engaging student learning in cooking the foods they have grown in the garden. Each schoolyard supports multiple gardening activities such as planting, tending, and harvesting seasonal herbs, fruits, and vegetables; composting food waste; and raising chickens. In addition, each edible schoolyard also has a dedicated kitchen. In the kitchen, students learn to prepare, cook, and eat the foods they cultivate in the garden. Foods prepared in the kitchen reflect the region's cultural diversity, which includes Hispanic, Punjabi, and African traditions. In addition to dedicated staff supporting facilities and teaching in the gardens and kitchens, curriculum and instruction are articulated with subject-area classroom teachers.

Each school therefore has its own ecological system of teaching and learning designed around, interacting with, and growing through the gardens, kitchens, and classrooms. In essence then, our study takes a multi-embedded case study approach with four distinct schools all embedded within the same philosophic and support network (Yin, 2018). Students participate in an average of 70 minutes of garden and kitchen activity every three weeks. Garden and kitchen activities are supported by dedicated staff, with financial assistance from a local non-profit educational organization whose answer to the question, "What is an Edible Schoolyard?," succinctly described the student experience:

> The Edible Schoolyard Kern County (ESYKC) provides students from across Kern County with a hands-on, sensory educational experience like nothing else.
>
> Academic concepts are brought to life, and students are able to make the connections between food, the environment, and wellness.
>
> In the garden, students cultivate the soil, plant seeds, and watch them grow every season. They are taught the principles necessary to grow their own food and learn how to maintain an ecosystem that fosters both healthy habits and environments. In turn, our gardens thrive seasonally and function with the assistance of the children who attend ESYKC programs.

> Their education continues in the kitchen, where students learn how to safely prepare recipes that are both nutritious and delicious, using fresh, healthy foods grown in our gardens.
>
> We encourage students to explore and awaken their senses to the world around them and to enjoy and appreciate food through seed to table education. (Edible Schoolyard Kern County, 2024)

The dedicated staff work with regular classroom teachers and after-school program coordinators to provide co-curricular and extracurricular activities. All four schools serve significant populations of traditionally underserved and marginalized students and encompass rural, suburban, and urban settings. School demographic information demonstrating similarities and differences is provided in Table 3.1.

School	Grades Served	Total Enrollment	Socioeconomically Disadvantaged	English Learners	Foster Youth	Location	Charter
School A	K-8	795	90.7%	42%	0%	Rural	Yes
School B	K-8	784	80.1%	22.6%	0%	Rural	Yes
School C	K-6	717	66.7%	11.4%	0.7%	Suburban	No
School D	K-6	757	93.1%	32.6%	1.3%	Urban	No

TABLE 3.1. School Demographics

While the schools share key demographic similarities, they also represent structural differences, most obviously in the rural, urban, and suburban settings represented, but also in other factors. Two schools, the urban and the suburban schools, are traditional elementary schools situated within two different larger school districts. These schools had their edible schoolyards added to the facilities long after they were first built. The original edible schoolyard in the region was located at the school in the suburban setting. This school has its edible schoolyard located across the street from the main school building. The urban school re-purposed an existing playground into their edible schoolyard, much as Alice Waters did in designing the edible schoolyard at Martin Luther King, Jr. Middle School in Berkeley. Indeed, Waters' edible schoolyard serves as the model for these schools located several hours south in California's Southern San Joaquin Valley. The remaining two schools, both in rural areas, are charter schools belonging to the same charter school network which intentionally seeks to incorporate edible schoolyards into the region's schools. Like the two regular public schools in the study with edible schoolyards, the charter network is closely affiliated with a local educational foundation seeking to promote edible schoolyards. The two charter schools were intentionally designed around the school garden, with an acre-sized garden literally in the middle of each school property, and with the kitchen and classrooms encircling the garden.

As Dewey envisioned school gardens over a century ago and reformers in the decades since have planted their own visionary garden seeds, the stakeholders in this modern expression of gardening and culinary education started with a vision. Primarily, the vision grew from the interest in edible schoolyards inspired by Alice Waters' work in Berkeley and brought to California's Southern Central Valley through the Grimm Family Education Foundation, a non-profit organization in Bakersfield. The foundation's vision statement captures the sentiment of modern edible schoolyard proponents by emphasizing expanded education opportunities, particularly for traditionally underserved students, and taking a holistic approach to student success by promoting wellness so that all will thrive and be successful in school and life (Grimm Family, 2024). The Grimm Family Education Foundation's mission statement even more clearly captures Dewey's and Waters' influences:

> [We are] [h]elping make vibrant communities in Kern County with our charter schools and Edible Schoolyard programs by closing the achievement gap, improving the health of students and families, and creating economic growth in the communities that we serve. By being fiscally responsible and innovative, we will broaden community impact through our programs, partnerships, research, fund development, and community outreach. (2024)

Student health is emphasized here but, as with Dewey, there is also a connection between the gardens' and kitchens' impact on student health with an emphasis on broader academic and community growth. This vision grows into reality in many ways, as will be explored through the remaining chapters, but a first blossom of insight can come from Damian, a garden educator at the urban school in our study. The school is located in a poverty-stricken area, as noted by both Damian and the school's principal in their conversations with us and symbolized by the graffiti and homeless people in the park right across the street. Yet, Damian noted that respect for the school garden is community-wide. There is evidence that the nearby homeless utilize the garden facilities at night and on weekends from some materials being rearranged in the greenhouse. The greenhouse sinks are likewise utilized after-hours. The garden staff do not lock the greenhouse doors. Yet, there is no graffiti and no theft. Well, for some reason, garden hoses are stolen from time to time, but otherwise, the school garden facility remains a safe and special space for students and community alike. Indeed, Kylie, the school principal, shared her surprise at the low rates of discipline among students at the school despite the school's rough reputation, a reality she attributes to the edible schoolyard.

Moving Forward

The remaining chapters provide further insights into creating the special and safe places of edible schoolyards. In the next chapter, we present student survey data to explore the students' perceptions of their garden and kitchen experiences, making connections to self-determination theory as a modern means to quantitatively explore Deweyan concepts of student autonomy, competence, and relatedness. We then proceed to draw from two dozen semi-structured interviews featuring a diversity of perspectives from educators involved in edible schoolyards including garden educators, kitchen educators, classroom teachers, a special education teacher, academic coaches, program managers, principals, a program director emphasizing curriculum development, and a CEO. Our participants are all directly involved in the work of edible schoolyards and represent a diversity of personal backgrounds including Mexican-American, Hispanic, Latina, Bi-Racial, African-American, Filipino, Korean, and white. Some have college degrees and state-approved teaching credentials; some emphasize their real-world experience. At least a half-dozen of the educators have enrolled their own children in the schools at which they teach. A similar number are first- or second-generation Americans having immigrated to this country themselves or were born here after their parents made the journey. They range in age from their twenties to their seventies and have been in education from a few years to many decades. All share a passion and a vision for edible schoolyard education.

Their passion leads to many participant stories. A grounded approach (Creswell & Poth, 2018) is taken in presenting the participants' stories using their own words as much as possible to illustrate their experiences, values, and perceptions of their work with students in the edible schoolyards.

Analysis was aided by Delve software and took a primarily inductive *in-vivo* approach as we sought themes utilizing the participants' own words. While all the participants were excited about edible schoolyard education and were eager to share their stories, we did change participant names per institutional review board (IRB) protocol. However, in doing so, I also hope the relative anonymity might help move the stories beyond the limits of these cases' time and place as readers engage in and recognize their own visions for more authentic and engaging educational experiences. To this end, I cover leadership stories in Chapter 5, continue with favorite engaging lessons in Chapter 6, make connections between the edible schoolyards and regular classrooms in Chapter 7, and provide ideas for starting a new edible schoolyard in Chapter 8. However, as students should be the center of the school experience, let us first turn to student perceptions of their edible schoolyard experiences in the next chapter.

References

Apple, M. W. (2005). Doing things the 'right' way: Legitimating educational inequalities in conservative times. *Educational Review, 57*(3), 271–293. https://doi.org/10.1080/00131910500149002

Apple, M. W. (2014). *Official knowledge: Democratic education in a conservative age* (3rd ed.). Routledge.

Apple, M. W. (2018). *The struggle for democracy in education: Lessons from social realities.* Routledge.

Atchoarena, D., & Gasperini, L. (2004). *Education for rural development: Towards new policy responses.* Food and Agriculture Organization of the United Nations and United Nations Educational, Scientific and Cultural Organization.

Blair, D. (2009). The child in the garden: An evaluative review of the benefits of school gardening. *The Journal of Environmental Education, 40*(2), 15–38. https://doi.org/10.3200/JOEE.40. 2.15-38

Canaris, I. (1995). Growing foods for growing minds: Integrating gardening and nutrition education into the total curriculum. *Children's Environments, 12*(2), 264–270. https://www.jstor.org/stable/41503435

Carson, R. (1962). *Silent spring*. Houghton Mifflin.

Creswell, J. W., & Poth, C. N. (2018). *Qualitative inquiry & research design: Choosing among five approaches* (4th ed.). SAGE.

Dale, R. (1999). Specifying globalization effects on national policy: A focus on mechanisms. *Journal of Educational Policy, 14*(1), 1–17. http://dx.doi.org/10.1080/026809399286468

Davis, J. N., Nikah, K., Landry, M. J., Vandyousefi, S., Ghaddar, R., Jeans, M., Hockett Cooper, M., Martin, B., Waugh, L., Sharma, S. V., & van den Berg, A. E. (2023). Effects of a school-based garden program on academic performance: A cluster of randomized controlled trial. *Journal of the Academcy of Nutrition and Dietetic, 123*(4), 637–642. https://doi.org/10.1016/j.jand.2022.08.125

Desmond, D., Grieshop, J., & Subramaniam, A. (2002). *Revisiting garden-based learning in basic education.* Food and Agriculture Organization of the United Nations and International Institute for Educational Planning.

Dewey, J., & Dewey, E. (1962). *Schools of tomorrow.* E. P. Dutton & Co., Inc. (Original work published 1915).

Duncan, D. W., Collins, A., Fuhrman, N. E., Knauft, D. A., & Berle, D. C. (2016). The impacts of a school garden program on urban middle school youth. *Journal of Agricultural Education, 57*(4), 174–185. https://doi.org/10.5032/jae.2016.04174

Dyg, P. M., & Wistoft, K. (2016). Wellbeing in school gardens: The case of the Gardens for Bellies food and environmental educational program. *Environmental Education Research, 24*(8), 1177–1191. https://doi.org/10.1080/13504622.2018.1434869

The Edible Schoolyard. (2024, January 30). *The Edible Schoolyard.* https://edibleschoolyard.org/about-us

Edible Schoolyard Kern County. (2024, February 13). *About Us – Edible Schoolyard Kern County.* https://esykerncounty.org/about-us/#our-mission

Fakharzadeh, S. (2015). Food for thought: The intersection of gardens, education, and community at Edible School Yard New Orleans. *Children, Youth, and Environments, 25*(3), 175–187. https://www.jstor.org/stable/10.7721/chilyoutenvi.25.3.0175

Food and Agriculture Organization of the United Nations. (2004). *School Gardens Concept Note: Improving Child Nutrition and Education through the Promotion of School Garden Programmes.* https://www.fao.org/4/af080e/af080e00.pdf

Foster, W. P. (2004). The decline of the local: A challenge to educational leadership. *Educational Administration Quarterly, 40*, 176–191. https://doi.org/10.1177/0013161X03260360

Glenn, J. L. (2000). *Environment-based education: Creating high performance schools and students.* National Environmental Education and Training Foundation.

Graham, H., Beall, D. L., Lussier, M., McLaughlin, P., & Zidenberg-Cherr, S. (2005). Use of school gardens in academic instruction. *Journal of Nutrition Education and Behavior, 37*(3), 147–151.

Grimm Family Education Foundation. (2024, February 13). *Homepage.* https://www.grimmeducation.org/

Huys, N., De Cocker, K., De Craemer, M., Roesbeke, M., Cardon, G., & De Lepeleere, S. (2017) School gardens: A qualitative study on implementation practices. *International Journal of Environmental Research and Public Health, 14*(2), 1454. https://doi.org/10.3390/ijerph14121454

Jagiello, M., Malkusz, G., & Szostek, S. (2021). School and kindergarten gardens as a place of education. History and contemporary design trends. *Architectus*, 2(66), 27–38. https://doi.org/10.37190/arc210203

Kipfer, H. J. (2018). *Gaining consensus on implementation, sustainability, and benefits of school garden programming in Washington, D.C.* (Publication No. 10845265) [Doctoral dissertation, College of Physical Activity and Sport Sciences at West Virginia University]. ProQuest Dissertations and Thesis Global.

Knoll, M. (2022). *Beyond rhetoric: New perspectives on John Dewey's pedagogy*. International Academic Publishers.

Kohlstedt, S. G. (2008). "A better crop of boys and girls": The school gardening movement, 1890-1920. *History of Education Quarterly, 48*(1), 58–93. https://doi.org/10.1111/j.17485959.2008.00126.x

Koyama, J. (2013). Global scare tactics and the call for US schools to be held accountable. *American Journal of Education 120*(1). http://www.jstor.org/stable/10.1086/673122

Monferrer, L., Lorenzo-Valentín, G., & Santágueda-Villanueva, M. (2022). Mathematical and experiential science education from the school garden: A review of the literature and recommendations for practice. *Education Sciences, 12*(47), 1–14. https://doi.org/10.3390/educsci12010047

Moore, R. C. (1995). Children gardening: First steps towards a sustainable future. *Children's Environments, 12*(2), 222–232. https://www.jstor.org/stable/41503430

Ohly, H., Gentry, S., Wigglesworth, R., Bethel, A., Lovell, R., & Garside, R. (2016). A systematic review of the health and well-being impacts of school gardening: Synthesis of quantitative and qualitative evidence. *BMC Public Health, 16*(1), 1–36. https://doi.org/10.1186/s12889-016-2941-0

Ozer, E. J. (2007). The effects of school gardens on students and schools: Conceptualization and considerations for maximizing healthy development. *Health Education & Behavior, 34*(6), 846–863. https://doi.org/10.1177/1090198106289002

Rahm, J. (2002). Emergent learning opportunities in an inner-city youth gardening program. *Journal of Research in Science Teaching, 39*(2), 164–184. https://doi.org/10.1002/tea.10015

Ratcliffe, M. M., Merrigan, K. A., Rogers, B. L., & Goldberg, J. P. (2011). The effects of school garden experiences on middle school-aged students' knowledge, attitudes, and behaviors associated with vegetable consumption. *Health Promotion Practice, 12*(1), 36–43. https://doi.org/10.1177/1524839909349182

Ray, R., Fisher, D. R., & Fisher-Maltese, C. (2016). School gardens in the city: Does environmental equity help close the achievement gap? *Du Bois Review, 13*(2), 379–395. https://doi.org/10.1017/S1742058X16000229

Schirmer, E. B., & Apple, M. W. (2016). Teachers, school boards, and the power of money: How the right wins at the local level. *The Educational Forum, 80*(2), 137–153. https://doi.org/10.1080/00131725.2016.1135384

Skinner, E. A., Chi, U., & The Learning-Gardens Educational Assessment Group (2012). Intrinsic motivation and engagement as "active ingredients" in garden-based education: Examining models and measures derived from self-determination theory. *The Journal of Environmental Education, 43*(1), 16–36. https://doi.org/10.1080/00958964.2011.596856

Stewart, I. T., Purner, E. K., Guzman, P. D. (2013). Socioeconomic disparities in the provision of school gardens in Santa Clara County, California. *Children, Youth, and Environments, 23*(2), 127–153. https://www.jstor.org/stable/10.7721/chilyoutenvi.23.2.0127

Szolowicz, M. A. (2020). Opposing versus supporting opting out of standardized testing: Policy subjectivity in the state legislative process. *The SoJo Journal: Educational Foundations and Social Justice Education, 6*(1–2), 97–112.

Szolowicz, M. A. (2021). Disassembling efforts to legalize opting-out in Arizona: A case study of legislative politics. *Teachers College Record, 123*(5), 1–22. https://doi.org/10.1177/016146812112300511

Tenuto, P. L. (2014). Advancing leadership: A model for cultivating democratic professional practice in education. *SAGE Open*, *4*(2), 1–13. https://doi.org/10.1177/2158244014530729

Trelstad, B. (1997). Little machines in their gardens: A history of school gardens in America, 1891 to 1920. *Landscape Journal, 16*(2), 161–173. https://www.jstor.org/stable/43323438

Wake, S. J. (2015, June). 'Same, same, but different': A comparison of rationales between historic and contemporary school garden development. In M. Ignatieva (Ed.), *Proceedings of the 52nd World Congress of the International Federation of Landscape Architects: History of the Future* (pp. 666–671). https://hdl.handle.net/10652/3373

Waters, A. (2008). *Edible schoolyard: A universal idea.* Chronicle Books.

Williams, D. R., & Dixon, P. S. (2013). Impact of garden-based learning on academic outcomes in schools: Synthesis of research between 1990 and 2010. *Review of Educational Research, 83*(2), 211–235. https://doi.org/10.3102/0034654313475824

Yin, R. K. (2018). *Case study research and applications: Designs and methods* (6th ed.). SAGE Publications, Inc.

Ylimaki, R. (2011). *Critical curriculum leadership: A framework for progressive education.* Routledge.

Ylimaki, R. M. (2012). Curriculum leadership in a conservative era. *Educational Administration Quarterly, 48*(2), 304–346. https://doi.org/10.1177/0013161X11427393

CHAPTER FOUR

SELF-DETERMINATION THEORY AND EDIBLE SCHOOLYARDS

As Dewey hoped, school gardens have become more prevalent as a feature of the modern school facility. In California alone, for example, the number has grown in recent years, from over 2,000 in 2007 (Ozer, 2007) to over 4,000 just three years later in 2010 (California Department of Education, 2010). The reasons justifying this growth are many, but four key factors tend to include 1) supporting academic performance—especially in the sciences, 2) teaching ecologically sustainable behaviors (think composting and recycling), 3) teaching knowledge of nutrition and healthy eating, and 4) supporting positive youth development (Skinner et al., 2012). Factors such as these have supported the adoption of schoolyard gardens in Kern County, as well, in both charter school academies and regular public schools. These schools form the focus on this study and will be explored in more depth through the remainder of this book. The question, of course, is whether these gardens are living up to the expectations that drove their establishment.

Further research has found clear evidence that student involvement in schoolyard gardens provides a number of positive outcomes for students, as individuals, including *student engagement* (Passy, 2014), serving as an effective *tool to confront the growing problem of childhood obesity* (Hazzad et al., 2011) by *building student nutritional knowledge* (2011) and by *increasing student physical activity* (Rees-Punia et al., 2017), and also *increasing student well-being* (Dyg & Wistoft, 2016). These positive outcomes are in addition to the academic advantages noted earlier. What may explain these positive outcomes? The answer likely lies in understanding the effects of intrinsic motivation.

Intrinsic motivation refers to the drive to accomplish a task for the simple joy and sense of accomplishment in doing the task, or satisfying internal needs (Vandeveer & Menefee, 2010). In a further development of this basic idea, Deci and Ryan (1985) developed self-determination theory (SDT) to explain the power of doing things that one wants to do, as opposed to doing those things that one is told to do. The Learning-Gardens Educational Assessment Group at Portland State University in Oregon applied this theory to education to suggest that schoolyard gardens are a way to ignite student motivation to learn by engaging students in fun learning activities outside, in the garden (Skinner et al., 2012). The researchers there suggest that the positive outcomes seen in their sample population (6th and 7th graders) are due to the relatedness, competence, and autonomy (the building blocks of SDT) that are provided for via the experiences that students get by working in the schoolyard gardens (Skinner et al., 2012, p. 20).

Self-determination theory is effective at providing a more modern and quantifiable way to explore the application and effects of Dewey's ideas in real schools. In doing so, we are continuing Dewey's work in approaching education through the scientific method, applying our own inquiry to systematically explore the relationship between students and their work, much like Dewey did through the establishment of his Laboratory School (e.g., Dewey 1915/2010, 1916/2016, 1938/2007). Philosophically, SDT, as expressed by Ryan and Deci (2017), deeply connects with Deweyan themes:

> Children learn more than reading, writing, and math in school. They also learn authority, industry, social relationships, and how they are valued and perceived by others outside the home. Schools shape the development of the whole child, affecting intellectual outcomes as well as motivation, self-concept, and the vitality and integrity of self-development. We should therefore consider that the hope and promise of schools is not only that they enable and enhance cognitive learning and growth in specific subject areas such as science, technology, engineering, and mathematics (STEM), but also that they facilitate the development of high-quality motivation, engagement, participation, citizenship, and social-emotional well-being. (Ryan & Deci, 2017, p. 353)

That children should not just learn academics but also flourish in schools is a prime objective of Ryan, Deci, and Dewey alike.

SDT captures key Deweyan themes, first and foremost by focusing on the student as an individual, such as is seen in the SDT concepts of autonomy and competence. Autonomy suggests that one's behaviors are self-endorsed or congruent with one's authentic interests and values. Competence suggests the feeling of being able, and the actual ability, to operate effectively within important life contexts. As with Dewey's vision, however, SDT does not end with the autonomous student, but recognizes the need for the individual to exist and function within a social environment that includes family, school, community, and nation. SDT's third significant concept is relatedness, or how the individual connects to and functions with others (Ryan & Deci, 2017).

Noting, as did Dewey, that the most powerful form of motivation is intrinsic (Ryan & Deci, 2000), these researchers also work on an organismic integration of development that envisions actors as being able to internalize extrinsic motivators (Deci & Ryan, 1985). The basic process through which SDT operates begins in a context of relationships in which rewards and feedback are experienced and develops as cognitive evaluations are made of sufficient competence to move forward and feelings of freedom of choice are experienced (Ryan & Deci, 2000). The researchers noted that "environments that provide optimal challenge, competence-promoting feedback, and support for autonomous activity will facilitate intrinsic motivation" (Deci & Ryan, 1985, p. 122). In addition to the purely intrinsic forms of motivation, Ryan and Deci also suggest that even some external motivators can be internalized. This is possible if the external motivators can be either identified as personally important or can be integrated (assimilated) into one's system of values (Ryan & Deci, 2000).

Therefore, to build upon Dewey's vision using modern quantifiable means, this study is grounded in the work of Ryan and Deci (2000, 2017) on self-determination theory (SDT). SDT has been utilized in prior work on school gardens (Skinner et al., 2012), as well as in business and community settings. SDT provides measurable categories of competence, autonomy, and relatedness that encapsulate Dewey's vision of the garden as providing an experiential means for students to grow in their academics while also developing as citizens related to the broader school, business, and civic communities. Ryan and Deci's (2017) three categories are further defined in Table 4.1.

Category	Definition
Competence	Feeling of operating effectively within one's important life contexts.
Autonomy	That one's behaviors are self-endorsed, or congruent with one's authentic interests and values.
Relatedness	Feeling socially connected and usually occurring when feeling cared for by others. Equally important is feeling that one is giving or contributing to others.

TABLE 4.1. Self-Determination Theory Categories

I hypothesize that the authentic activities experienced in the school gardens, coupled with the experiences of cooking and eating what is grown, will relate to feelings of competence, autonomy, and relatedness. SDT allows us to hypothesize that the intrinsic motivation developed in the gardens and kitchens will facilitate improved student engagement, with positive implications for students' perceptions of their abilities.

To explore the student perceptions of their garden and kitchen experiences, we surveyed about 1,000 students across four schools, each featuring one-acre school gardens and accompanying kitchens. The survey, adapted from the work of Skinner et al. (2012) on school gardens, shows strong psychometric properties. The survey asked students to report their level of agreement with statements such as, "being in the Edible Schoolyard Garden helps me understand science." For this and other statements, students reported whether the statement was "not at all true," "a little bit true," "somewhat true," "fairly true," or "totally true," for 48 questions. Surveys were administered via Google Forms during regular classroom time in December 2022 and again at the end of the same schoolyear, in May 2023. Survey results were then analyzed, first for descriptive statistics, and subsequently for bi-variate correlations between survey questions and self-determination theory categories. Spearman's rho was utilized due to the method's appropriateness for nominal data, particularly Likert scales as utilized in the survey. All correlations were conducted using SPSS version 28.0.0.0.

Correlations were run for all four schools as a group and then separately for each school individually. Further, correlations were run for relationships between individual survey questions, but also between individual questions and the sum score for questions within a category: competence, autonomy, and relatedness. Within the survey, some questions were viewed as having a "totally true" (or a 5 on the Likert Scale) as the desirable score and were considered positive questions. Others, for control purposes, were designed as having a negatively desirable score of "not at all true" (or a 1 on the Likert scale). Examples of positive intended questions included, "being in the edible schoolyard garden helps me understand science," while negatively intended control questions included, "I don't have the brains to garden." Positive questions, not the control questions, were used to create the sum score for each student in each SDT category. Essentially, we were looking to see if all questions were equally correlated to the sum or if certain questions, and thus experiences, were more strongly correlated to student perceptions of competence, autonomy, and relatedness.

Similarly, for the descriptive statistics, self-determination categories were determined first by creating an ideal score composed of the number of positive questions in the category multiplied by the top Likert score of 5. The average sum of the student responses for each category was then divided by the ideal sum to determine a percentage of the ideal achieved. For both the descriptive and correlative portions, a strong result ranges from .80 to 1.00, a strong moderate result from .70 to .79, a moderate result from .50 to .69, a weak moderate result from .40 to .49, and a weak result from .0 to .39.

Findings

Table 4.2 shows survey results from Fall 2022 that demonstrate moderate to strongly moderate findings regarding students' perceptions of competence, autonomy, and relatedness. In all four schools individually, and together as a whole, students reported moderate perceptions of competence as represented by the "All Schools" score of 66.15%. Regarding autonomy and relatedness, students reported strongly moderate perceptions based on their garden and kitchen experiences of about 71%.

One semester later, student perceptions increased, as shown in Table 4.3. Competence remains the lowest of the three; however, the "All Schools" selection representatively increased from a moderate 66.15% to a strongly moderate 74.65%.

The changes are further presented in Table 4.4. Autonomy and relatedness both grew into the strong category with results of 80.29% and 83.15%, respectively. The only outlier is seen for School D, which saw a small decrease in the areas of competence and autonomy.

School	Grades Included	n =	Competence	Autonomy	Relatedness
All Schools	3-6	907	39.69 66.15%	46.19 71.06%	39.43 71.69%
School A	3-6	293	38.55 64.25%	44.29 68.14%	38.36 69.75%
School B	3-6	287	39.98 66.63%	46.58 71.66%	39.73 72.24%
School C	3-6	277	40.36 67.27%	47.64 73.29%	40.25 73.18%
School D	3-6	50	40.92 68.20%	47.06 72.40%	39.34 71.52%

TABLE 4.2. Student Survey Results for Positive Self-Determination Categories, Fall 2022

School	Grades Included	n =	Competence	Autonomy	Relatedness
All Schools	3-6	992	44.79 74.65%	52.19 80.29%	45.73 83.15%
School A	3-6	354	43.75 72.92%	49.42 76.03%	4436 80.65%
School B	3-6	320	47.10 78.50%	55.02 84.65%	47.28 85.96%
School C	3-6	246	43.84 73.07%	53.36 82.09%	46.43 84.42%
School D	4-6	58	39.95 66.58%	45.95 70.69%	41.02 74.58%

TABLE 4.3. Student Survey Results for Positive Self-Determination Categories, Spring 2023

By the end of the school year, regular experiences in the gardens and kitchens resulted in stronger student perceptions of their own competence, autonomy, and relatedness. However, are all experiences in the gardens and kitchens equal in relation to these overall student perceptions? Using a Spearman rho correlation, student responses to individual questions in each category were correlated to their sum score of the positive responses. There was variation in the strength of the correlations, suggesting a variation in experiences.

School	Competence	Autonomy	Relatedness
All Schools	+8.50 points 11.39% change	+9.23 points 11.50% change	+11.46 points 13.78% change
School A	+8.67 points 11.89% change	+7.89 10.38% change	+10.90 13.52% change
School B	+11.87 points 15.12% change	+12.99 15.35% change	+13.72 15.96% change
School C	+5.80 points 7.94% change	+8.80 10.72% change	+11.24 13.31% change
School D	-1.62 points -2.43% change	-0.02 -3.00% change	+3.06% 4.10% change

TABLE 4.4. Change in Percentage Point Results from Fall 2022 to Spring 2023

The three strongest correlations for each school and the schools combined are presented in Table 4.5 (competence), Table 4.6 (autonomy), and Table 4.7 (relatedness). Across the four schools, several student perceptions stand out. Students consistently reported that they learn how to do science, including experimenting, measuring, observing, and finding new facts, as related to their perceptions of competence. Students consistently reported the gardens as being fun and enjoyable places, which relates to their feelings of autonomy. Seeing things grow and learning important things in the gardens and kitchens also relate to their perceptions of autonomy. The garden and kitchen experiences relate to students' positive relationship with their school, and they feel these spaces are good places.

Students from all schools reported confidence in their ability to do science, including experimenting, measuring, and observing new facts as the most significant areas of competence, or the feeling of operating effectively within their important life contexts from their work in the gardens. Many students, notably in schools B and D, also reported similar findings from their work in the kitchens. Also notable are the feelings of being pretty good at gardening and being able to make gardens grow. Interestingly, students from School D reported cross-cultural connections as they learned what people from other cultures grow and eat, suggesting the social applicability of garden experiences.

School	Survey Question	Correlation to Student Category Sum Score
All Schools	I learned how to do science—experimenting, measuring, observing, finding new facts (in the garden) I am an important part of making the gardens better I learned how I can treat the environment better	$r_s = .722, p < .001$ $r_s = .659, p < .001$ $r_s = .647, p < .001$
School A	I learned how to do science—experimenting, measuring, observing, finding new facts (in the garden) I learned how I can treat the environment better I am pretty good at gardening	$r_s = .740, p < .001$ $r_s = .671, p < .001$ $r_s = .667, p < .001$
School B	I learned how to do science—experimenting, measuring, observing, finding new facts (in the garden) I am pretty good at gardening I learned how to do science—experimenting, measuring, observing, finding new facts (in the kitchen)	$r_s = .699, p < .001$ $r_s = .653, p < .001$ $r_s = .624, p < .001$
School C	I learned how to do science—experimenting, measuring, observing, finding new facts (in the garden) I am an important part of making the gardens better I feel at home in the Learning Gardens	$r_s = .774, p < .001$ $r_s = .680, p < .001$ $r_s = .668, p < .001$
School D	I learned what other people from other cultures grow and eat I learned how to do science—experimenting, measuring, observing, finding out new facts (in the kitchen) I learned how to do science—experimenting, measuring, observing, finding out new facts (in the garden)	$r_s = .747, p < .001$ $r_s = .734, p < .001$ $r_s = .724, p < .001$

TABLE 4.5. Competence

Table 4.6 examines students' perceptions of their own autonomy, or how their behaviors and experiences are congruent with their own interests and values. Here, students consistently reported that gardening is "fun," and that they "enjoy it." They also suggest the academic usefulness of the garden and kitchen experiences by suggesting they garden "so [they] can learn important things" and acknowledging the coolness of seeing things grow. The cool factor suggests the possibility of crossover learning from the garden and kitchen to the regular classroom, which we will explore in more depth in Chapter 7.

Table 4.7 explores relatedness, or the feelings of being socially connected. Ryan and Deci (2017) further suggest that relatedness usually occurs when people feel cared for by others. Feelings of being able to give or contribute to others also play into feelings of relatedness. Through their garden and kitchen experiences, students consistently reported they felt they were doing something good for their school. That school for these primary grade students forms their main form of community, the social connections

School	Survey Question	Correlation to Student Category Sum Score
All Schools	Why do I garden? It's fun Why do I garden? I enjoy it Why do I garden? So I can learn important things	$r_s = .801, p < .001$ $r_s = .795, p < .001$ $r_s = .784, p < .001$
School A	Why do I garden? I enjoy it Why do I garden? It's fun Why do I garden? So I can learn important things	$r_s = .821, p < .001$ $r_s = .815, p < .001$ $r_s = .808, p < .001$
School B	Why do I garden? It's fun Why do I garden? So I can learn important things Why do I garden? It's cool to see things grow	$r_s = .736, p < .001$ $r_s = .732, p < .001$ $r_s = .723, p < .001$
School C	Gardening is interesting It's cool to see things grow Why do I garden? So I can learn important things	$r_s = .799, p < .001$ $r_s = .732, p < .001$ $r_s = .723, p < .001$
School D	Why do I garden? I enjoy it It's cool to see things grow Why do I garden? It's fun	$r_s = .889, p < .001$ $r_s = .883, p < .001$ $r_s = .873, p < .001$

TABLE 4.6. Autonomy

School	Survey Question	Correlation to Student Category Sum Score
All Schools	It makes me feel like I'm doing something good for the school The Learning Garden is a good place for students like me I feel like a real part of the Learning Gardens	$r_s = .786, p < .001$ $r_s = .723, p < .001$ $r_s = .722, p < .001$
School A	It makes me feel like I'm doing something good for my school I feel like we are doing something good for the environment The Learning Gardens is a good place for students like me	$r_s = .804, p < .001$ $r_s = .756, p < .001$ $r_s = .712, p < .001$
School B	It makes me feel like I'm doing something good for my school The Learning Gardens is a good place for students like me I feel like a part of the Learning Gardens	$r_s = .755, p < .001$ $r_s = .729, p < .001$ $r_s = .712, p < .001$
School C	I feel like a real part of the Learning Gardens It makes me feel like I'm doing something good for my school I feel good	$r_s = .766, p < .001$ $r_s = .763, p < .001$ $r_s = .701, p < .001$
School D	It makes me feel like I'm doing something good for my school The Learning Garden makes our school special I feel good	$r_s = .884, p < .001$ $r_s = .836, p < .001$ $r_s = .833, p < .001$

TABLE 4.7. Relatedness

made through the gardens and kitchens suggest the experiences' usefulness in achieving a key social aim of education, to operate effectively within a community. Students also consistently reported that they "feel good," and that the gardens and kitchens are "good places for students like [them]." Here, students may be suggesting they feel cared for and comfortable in the gardens and kitchens, as places that are good for them. While it is possible simply being in the natural setting of the garden and being in the kitchen producing nutritious food promotes these feelings, the educator's use of and priorities for the kitchens and gardens likely also promote these student perceptions. We will explore educator priorities in the chapter on leadership and provide further insights as we explore our favorite lessons.

Students experiencing gardens and kitchens report stronger perceptions of their own competence, autonomy, and relatedness to their school community over time. Students report that the experiences of science inherent in garden and kitchen activities are related to their overall feelings of competence. The fun and engaging activities relate to their sense of autonomy; their behaviors within the kitchen and garden experiences are congruent with their authentic interests. The kitchens and gardens further correlate to students' sense of relatedness, in that they feel socially connected and cared for within their school communities. Dewey envisioned the school garden and accompanying kitchen experiences as developing the whole child, including the child's academic capability and ability to connect to a broader society. Students participating in school gardens and kitchens today demonstrate this holistic growth, as suggested by our student survey results. How to achieve these results forms the remainder of this book. Further, as our methodology for the remaining chapters shifts from a quantitative to a qualitative approach based on interviews and observations, we promise there will be very little math moving forward.

References

California Department of Education (2010). School garden program overview: A healthy nutrition environment – Linking education, activity, and food through school gardens.

Deci, E. L., & Ryan, R. M. (1985). *Intrinsic motivation and self-determination in human behavior*. Plenum Press.

Dewey, J. (2007). *Experience and education*. Simon and Schuster. (Original work published 1938).

Dewey, J. (2010). *The school and society and the child and the curriculum* (2nd ed.). Digireads.com publishing. (Original work published 1915).

Dewey, J. (2016). *Democracy and education.* Ozymandias Press. (Original work published 1916).

Dyg, P. M., & Wistoft, K. (2016). Wellbeing in school gardens: The case of the Gardens for Bellies food and environmental educational program. *Environmental Education Research, 24*(8), 1177–1191. https://doi.org/10.1080/13504622.2018.1434869

Hazzard, E. L. (2011). *Utilization of garden-based education to positively impact children's nutrition knowledge and behaviors.* [Unpublished doctoral dissertation]. University of California, Davis.

Ozer, E. J. (2007). The effects of school gardens on students and schools: Conceptualization and considerations for maximizing healthy development. *Health Education & Behavior, 34*(6), 846–863. https://doi.org/10.1177/1090198106289002

Passy, R. (2014). School gardens: Teaching and learning outside the front door. *International Journal of Primary, Elementary, and Early Years Education, 42*(1), 22–38. https://doi.org/10.1080/03004279.2011.636371

Rees-Punia, E., Holloway, A., Knauft, D., & Schmidt, M. D. (2017). Effects of school gardening lessons on elementary school children's physical activity and sedentary time. *Journal of Physical Activity and Health, 14*, 959–964. https://doi.org/10.1123/jpah.2016-0725

Ryan, R. M., & Deci, E. L. (2000). Self-determination theory and the facilitation of intrinsic motivation, social development, and well-being. *American Psychologist, 55*(1), 68–78. https://doi.org/10.1037/0003-066X.55.1.68

Ryan, R. M., & Deci, E. L. (2017). *Self-determination theory*. The Guilford Press.

Skinner, E. A., Chi, U., & The Learning-Gardens Educational Assessment Group (2012). Intrinsic motivation and engagement as "active ingredients" in garden-based education: Examining models and measures derived from self-determination theory. *The Journal of Environmental Education, 43*(1), 16–36. https://doi.org/10.1080/00958964.2011.596856

Vandeveer, R. C., & Menefee, M. L. (2010). *Human Behavior in Organizations,* (2nd ed.). Pearson.

CHAPTER FIVE

LEADERSHIP FOR EDIBLE SCHOOLYARDS

I TEACH SEVERAL EDUCATIONAL leadership classes that encompass a variety of leadership roles, including preparing teacher leaders, principals, and superintendents. In my classes, I enjoy leading discussions regarding what actually constitutes leadership, and I particularly like to set up a dilemma or continuum between two competing definitions of prophets and leaders. Both prophets and leaders serve valuable functions in pointing the way toward a different and, hopefully, better future for the people in the schools and communities they serve. Yet, there is a distinct difference between the two roles (English, 2002). On the one hand, prophets have a clear vision of a different tomorrow, yet few people follow them. Prophets have a lonely existence, often marked by lengthy stays in the literal or figurative wilderness. Their visions often remain unrealized, although some may find prominence in future generations. On the other hand, leaders also possess a vision of a different future, but when they turn around on the pathway toward building that future, they find there are people behind and with them. In other words, leaders keep one foot firmly grounded in the realities of here and now even while taking a step forward. Leaders effect change in the real world, in the here and now.

By this measure, Dewey was much more of a prophet than a leader. His vision for education centered on the whole child and emphasized participatory experiences that authentically led to the knowledge and skills needed for effective citizenship in a democratic society. This vision was compelling at the turn of the 20th century and continues to be so to this day, well into the 21st. Yet, Dewey's own efforts at leading and administrating his school, the Laboratory School, were brief and ended ingloriously (Knoll, 2022). While Dewey was an acknowledged visionary, the work of leadership also requires attention to the school's finances, rules and regulations, course of study, and other management requirements. While Dewey talked extensively about democracy in his vision for education, in practice, he often was inaccessible, inconsiderate, and uncooperative with the faculty, staff, and parents whose collaboration was needed. Dewey actually managed his school by making decisions alone and in an uncompromising manner. Despite his powerful vision of participatory democracy, Dewey led as an isolated autocrat (Knoll, 2022).

Dewey seemed to realize he was more of a visionary prophet than an effective leader and administrator. In part, this realization is seen in Dewey's choices following his time as an administrator: He never returned to a significant executive role. His writings also provide insight into his priorities as a philosopher and visionary. Attention to key terms such as leadership and principal are missing in his significant writings such as *The School and Society and the Child and the Curriculum* (1915/2010), *Democracy and Education* (1916/2016), and the co-authored writing with his daughter Evelyn, *Schools of Tomorrow* (1915/1962). Yet, while specific attention to leadership as a concept rooted in the hierarchy of bureaucracy is missing, *Schools of Tomorrow* does address leadership through the work of mostly teachers and some principals who were effectively implementing his vision. For example, the Deweys (1915/1962) describe the role of the director and teachers in implementing a vision of nature study through the whole school organization at the Little School in the Woods in Greenwich, Connecticut. The school includes a garden, and the Deweys describe how the director created a vision for the school organization that encompassed experience in the things of nature while the teachers provided training through the nature study, including explaining what they were doing and calling attention to needed details.

By emphasizing in *Schools of Tomorrow* the vision of educator leaders in providing experiential education and then discussing the responsibilities of various roles within the school, such as principal and teacher, Dewey may have actually, and perhaps ironically, also provided a new vision of educational leadership that is both transformative and distributed. Hallinger (2003) provides a concise summary of both that emphasizes the connections between the two leadership models:

> Transformational leadership focuses on developing the organization's capacity to innovate. Rather than focusing specifically on direct coordination, control, and supervision of curriculum and instruction, transformational leadership seeks to build the organization's capacity to select its purposes and to support the development of changes to practices in teaching and learning. Transformational leadership may be viewed as distributed in that it focuses on developing a shared vision and shared commitment to school change. (p. 330)

The appropriateness of transformational leadership's emphasis on creating and implementing a new vision of education to Deweyan education should be clear. Rather than commanding and controlling, the transformative leaders set a vision of education, then work collaboratively with people to build that vision in the here and now. Capacity refers to the ability or power to get something done. The transformational leader recognizes that a new vision requires new capacities. For example, teachers may need training in new instructional approaches to better suit the garden and kitchen experiences. The garden and kitchen facilities themselves are part of the school's capacity, as the transformational leader will need to determine where these facilities will be built on the school grounds and find the money to build them. Yet, this transformative work is not done in isolation. Rather, the work is distributed among all members of the school organization, including administration, teachers, staff, and even parents and students. Transformational leadership is not limited to a formal bureaucratically-defined role such as principal, but is open to anyone seeking to engage others in developing and implementing a shared vision. While Dewey himself notably failed at this model of leadership, the educators' work described in *Schools of Tomorrow* inherently recognizes transformational and distributed leadership, even if the terms themselves will not become more thoroughly recognized in educational leadership studies until almost a century later (e.g., Bass et al., 1996; Canterino et al., 2020; Harris et al., 2007; Harris & DeFlammis, 2016; Leithwood & Jantzi, 2005; Liu et al., 2021; Moolenaar et al., 2010; Ylimaki, 2012).

The schools in this study all possess well-developed edible schoolyards, including one-acre gardens and accompanying kitchens. Our interest centers around the dual questions of who becomes engaged in edible schoolyard education and what they contribute to the vision of edible schoolyard education. The visionary aspect of edible schoolyard education emerges from our participants' motivations for joining the edible schoolyard movement and their hopes for what they want to accomplish for students. By talking to a variety of educators, including those who work specifically in the gardens, those who work specifically in the kitchens, those who work in regular classroom settings that interact with the gardens and kitchens, those in school-level administrative support roles, and those in more executive roles such as director and CEO, we recognize the distributed nature of leadership.

Edible Schoolyard Teachers

Garden Educators

The garden educators' work centers on the children in designing, implementing, and evaluating lessons in the school gardens. They, therefore, work directly with the students as teachers but also work closely with the Edible Schoolyard Foundation curriculum director in creating and implementing the garden experience that is shared across the school network. They also bear a great responsibility in prepping and maintaining the gardens, as not all work that needs to be done to cultivate a one-acre garden can be done in the time allotted to the young elementary school students. Some work, such as the maintenance of tools, might best be done by adults anyway, due to safety concerns. That said, the garden educators are proud that all tools used in the gardens are real tools. They do not use toys but rather have size- and age-appropriate real tools. As such, providing safety instructions and supervision form key aspects of the educators' roles. In our network of edible schoolyards, some garden educators are funded by the educational foundation. Others are funded through co-curricular and extra-curricular money provided by their schools and districts.

Jose—Garden Educator

Jose immigrated from Mexico, from a town so poor he had to ride a horse 30 minutes to school, to the Central Valley when he was 16 years old. As with many immigrants, he had nothing except the clothes on his back. He and his family took agricultural jobs, namely, picking in the fields. His family recognized the importance of education and offered him a choice: stay in the fields or go to school. Jose chose school. He attended the local community college for four years, learned English along the way, and joined MESA. A favorite teacher recognized his interest and aptitude in mathematics and encouraged him to apply to four-year universities, which led him to be accepted to California Polytechnic State University at San Luis Obispo. Cal Poly is one of the most prestigious schools in California if not the nation. Perhaps notably relevant to our story, Cal Poly has emphasized learning by doing as their primary pedagogy since 1901. There, Jose earned a bachelor's degree in electrical engineering which led to a job working on satellites for Northrup Grumman.

A trip back to Mexico where he met his wife, and their subsequent marriage, led the new family back to the rural community. There, Jose found work tutoring new immigrants in English with a non-profit organization. As the Grow School started in the community, Jose saw the community interest and saw opportunity to continue as a mentor encouraging a new generation of students to pursue college, as well, through the charter school. Further, he had memories of his childhood in rural Mexico where his family grew and cooked their own food. There was no supermarket in their hometown, leading the family, and everybody else, to grow their own food.

Yet, despite the agricultural riches of the Central Valley, the town where Jose and his wife settled was technically a food desert. Only one grocery store served the area, and it did not offer a broad selection of fresh ingredients. Jose was intrigued by the garden approach Grow offered as he was well aware from personal experience that healthy options were not often available at home, and his experience in Mexico showed him that in food deserts, growing and preparing your own food may be the only viable option for nutritious food. In one story, Jose recounted how the students grew kale, something that was not available in town and which most if not all had never tried, and started their kale harvest from tiny seeds the students planted themselves.

Jose sees the gardens as an opportunity to cultivate a college-going culture by providing experiences through which students learn and practice essential concepts such as life cycles along with key thinking skills such as comparison and contrast and pattern development. Jose also recalls the value of growing his own nutritious food in the food desert that was his rural town in Mexico and, perhaps ironically, sees the need for growing nutritious food in the food desert of his adopted town in the United States. Likewise, the kitchen educators, who personally or whose families recently immigrated from Mexico and the Philippines, have fond memories of gardening and cooking with their moms, tias (aunts), tios (uncles), and fathers. The gardens therefore become a place of warmth and welcome for newly arrived students to the strange land with its new language. By providing a familiar place, the gardens become a gateway to the education and opportunities America promises, as long as the planting of flowers, fruits, and vegetables is well integrated with academic concepts and skills.

Damian—Garden Educator

Damian is not a huge fan of technology. As a regular classroom teacher before taking on the role of garden educator, she rode the technology bandwagon for a while, attending conferences in San Francisco and incorporating Google Docs, Chromebooks, Wi-Fi, and even iPads into the classroom. But she noticed the kids were not really engaged in the struggle of learning. Other teachers were giving the kids their "binkies," or pacifiers in the form of iPads to keep them quiet and occupied but not necessarily learning. Damian wanted nothing to do with this electronic pacification of students and started looking for alternatives. The park across from the school was "dangerous." If the students in this urban school were going to have a safe space outside and away from technology, it was going to have to be at school. That was where the garden came in.

Her family were Okies, arriving in the region during the Dust Bowl, having lost their farm in Oklahoma in the 1930s. Her dad became a geologist in Bakersfield's other major economic engine, the oil industry, and worked directly in the oil fields. But she recalls fondly working the family garden at home, growing the family's own food, and recalls the challenge and struggle that came along with getting something to come to fruition. She believes this grit, my word, is key to learning, and the emphasis on technology today largely removes this by making things too easy and not forcing the kids to challenge themselves. The dirt of the garden offers an alternative, so Damian deliberately moved away from technology, first as a tutor and then, by happenstance of simply watching the district advertisements and seeing this opportunity arise, at the school garden.

Damian has a degree in public administration from the local state university, California State University, Bakersfield, which she pursued instead of business due to there being "less math." Yet this degree does still provide a sense of organizational needs, including budgeting. She noted that a district might spend $750,000 on training teachers for a reading program that they had purchased and noted this with a hint of disdain. Might some of this money be shifted, with a different vision from school leaders, into gardens and kitchens? In other words, there is money, and thinking about how to spend it differently might produce different results.

James—Garden Educator

Trauma has informed James' experience leading to the gardens, both his own and that of others. As an activity leader, he was drawn to sports, as it allowed kids an opportunity to triumph over trauma. He has seen kids compete and win despite broken homes. In one story, he watched a girl compete and really outdo her competitors in the long jump by "like 3 feet." On the drive home, he noticed she had a burn on her leg and asked about it. Apparently, the burn was from spilled overly hot soup, but if she could compete with that trauma, how much more could she compete if healthy? Regarding his own trauma, James was diagnosed with diabetes at 22 and had a heart attack at 26. When the job at the urban school came up, he thought that he could do it, as he had some experience and positive family memories gardening with his grandma when he was a child. Yet, he did not, by his own admission, have much experience, as he had not been in the garden in the intervening decades. When he started, he was literally going to the store to buy Miracle Grow, as he thought that is how you made things grow. He did, however, recognize his inexperience and set about educating himself through researching gardens.

James captures several themes we have seen with others: There is a deep-seated feeling of safety and productivity associated with childhood gardening memories that has drawn him to the edible gardens at school. He also has a genuine interest in helping kids and recreating these safe spaces he had experienced. It should be noted that he is at a school which has taken a very deliberately socio-emotional approach to the garden education, and James' story illustrates this approach. Further, James shows initiative, as have others, such as the parent who wanted a garden and then taught herself how to write grants and approach business and school communities for donations.

Health plays a key role in James' approach to the gardens, but the broad issue of health takes several forms: First, James is interested in the kids' personal health. The school is in a high-poverty urban environment. While set in the midst of the Southern San Joaquin Valley, one of the richest areas of food production on the planet and thus nicknamed America's Garden, the urban area is itself a food desert. People rely less on fresh vegetables and more on processed and canned food, in part due to cost, in part due to not having access to reliable resources including time and energy to prepare meals, and in part due to not knowing how to prepare foods. James' work provides an opportunity to work at least on the preparation end and maybe some on how to effectively utilize available resources for a healthier and tastier food experience. James is also interested in preparing kids for healthy living beyond school. He notes that there are good agricultural jobs available in the region that pay better than picking in the fields but also require greater knowledge of science, math, and literacy. So, his garden experiences focus on these concepts and skills, as well as incorporating experiential learning through rain catchers, composting, and recycling.

Lydia—Garden Educator

Lydia was inspired to get into education by her own first-grade teacher: "My first-grade teacher just walked on water. She was just the most amazing woman ever. And she is what made me want to be a teacher. I wanted to be that for students." Lydia was further inspired to pursue the biological sciences by another teacher in high school:

> And then in high school, I had a teacher that just blew my mind with marine biology, and so I entered college as a marine biologist. But about my sophomore year, I knew that wasn't really what I wanted. I was more of a people person. So, I switched to a liberal studies major and became a teacher.

Lydia's combination of content, interest in biology, focus on people, the inspiration from her own teachers, and her recognition of being a "people person" herself is not unusual for those working in the edible schoolyards. Lydia shares another experience with a notable number of other edible schoolyard teachers, in that she lived in Mexico for a while, although her experience was as an exchange student rather than the immigrant experience others in the edible schoolyards had:

> That's what got me into education. In terms of, you know, the question asked for moments in my own education that were impactful for me while I was in high school: I lived in Mexico as an exchange student, for a summer. And I had to navigate a foreign country with a language I didn't know at the time, I'd never been to, and that was a really pivotal time in my life in terms

> of learning who I was and how I function and becoming independent. . . . [T]-hat absolutely changed how I view learning new things. So that, I think, also helped me here towards education.

Lydia's exchange experience brought a new appreciation for the challenges students face, especially empathy for immigrant students arriving in a new country. The experience also contributed to her sense of authentic and engaging education. While immersed in a different country with different customs and a language that was different from her own, the everyday experiences of interacting with others contributed bit by bit to learning and growth, not unlike the way immersion in a garden might contribute to student learning in a different manner.

Lydia's position at her school is a sort of teacher on special assignment (TOSA) role in which she is responsible for planning, implementing, and evaluating a number of programs, particularly after-school programs. In her words, she had tremendous responsibility to ensure a variety of programs were working and also, "hey, can you make sure this little garden thing happens?" Overseeing all the programs was challenging, but she worked with extra diligence on the fledgling garden project by ordering supplies, materials, and tools, supervising the agricultural team to ensure they were creating lessons aligned with the vision for the school and garden, and serving as community liaison to spread the message of what they were doing and solicit community support.

The role of community liaison produced a cool community event, the school's own farmers market. Especially in the first year, they had no idea how much produce was going to be produced. Turns out, it was quite a bit even at the end of the first year, which included transition. In fall 2019, consistent with the "well, what do we do now?" grounded approach as their labors literally produced fruit (and vegetables), Lydia decided to act upon her role as community liaison by hosting a farmers market. They sold about ten different types of produce. They sold eggs the chickens had laid. And in true farmers market style, they supplemented the foodstuffs for sale with activities like face painting and some food vendors. The Condors, the beloved local minor league professional hockey team, also had a booth. While Lydia assumed responsibility for organizing the event, the students played an active role. Students had grown little seedlings of starter vegetables which they sold to community members to take home. The students also handled all the financial transactions, thus learning basic business, financial, and customer service skills in the process. Sadly, the COVID-19 pandemic prevented a repeat of the farmers market. Still, it was successful in Lydia's view, due to the community involvement and as measured by the fact that "everything sold out."

Valerie—Garden Educator

Valerie grew up gardening with her dad, married a farmer, and maintained her own garden at home. She had fond memories of gardening both alone and with others, such as time spent with her dad tending the fruit trees in their backyard, and she had a certain commitment to the gardening lifestyle. She is part Filipino, and these fond memories of family and gardening are similar to those we heard from others with first- and second-generation American experiences. Her connection to gardening as part of schooling came about more from an academic rather than experiential pathway, however. Valerie pursued a college degree in business but found herself reading about the history of the U.S. school system. In particular, she became fascinated with the experiential education that used to be offered in many American schools by way of such classes as carpentry and wood shop—classes that used to be offered in many American schools. Valerie noted, and we also saw in our own review of education in America, that farming at one time formed an accepted and needed goal of education, although farming fell out of favor with the urbanization and industrialization of the early 1900s. Still, she was inspired to emphasize learning about "the practical tools of life."

Valerie's direct connection to gardening and practical learning as part of schooling came about through her reading:

> I started reading more about education and just learning more about [its] history, [and] like I already touched on, it just really struck me that something I love to do and that I think is important could also be something very educational for my own kids.

This "aha moment" occurred for Valerie, as it did for other participants, because of life circumstances. In Valerie's case, she needed a job and was looking online for opportunities when she came across the Grow Schools ad. In her own "lightbulb" moment, she realized she could get paid for the work she was already engaged in and passionate about.

As Dewey perhaps envisioned when he discussed the garden as a starting point leading to other connections with academics in the schoolhouse and with the broader community, including business interests, Valerie leveraged her business degree with an emphasis in marketing to make the garden happen. She started out small, first combing the Internet for small grants. In the process, she learned how to be a grant writer as she applied for and got grants for a few hundred dollars here and a few hundred dollars there. She also worked the local businesses. Through the simple but tedious work of walking into stores, speaking with the managers, and asking for specific items, many donations were obtained.

It did help that Valerie already had connections to leverage through her husband's farm work, but she also leveraged her other community connections such as her church. In fact, her first fundraising was through friends at the church and led to the establishment of a GoFundMe account. Applying her business acumen to the startup project of a school garden, she emphasized clarity about what she was creating and what precisely was needed to make the garden happen. She emphasized small victories, such as a small herb garden, and then leveraged them into bigger grants and opportunities.

Kitchen Educators

The kitchen educators perform a very similar role to the garden educators in this well-developed edible schoolyard model. Like the garden educators, they focus on providing curriculum, instruction, and evaluation, but do so, obviously, in the kitchens rather than the gardens. They work closely with a director of curriculum and instruction from the Edible Schoolyard Foundation in these duties to create engaging lessons that focus on utilizing the fresh food grown in the gardens, and available from the local community, to prepare nutritious and hopefully delicious meals. Because gardens are very seasonal, and instruction needs to occur across seasons, the kitchens must also utilize fresh produce from local stores to supplement the garden's harvest. They also play a key role in safety, notably as seen in the kids' safe use of real knives. Also like the garden educators, they approached kitchen education from a variety of backgrounds and perspectives. Not all are credentialed teachers, as the charter school network and the districts for which they work approach the jobs from an enrichment or supplemental lens, at least as far as the finances are concerned. This allows the hiring of individuals who have a passion for edible schoolyards and kids' learning, while not being restrained by the extensive credentialing requirements. Diversity and an openness to innovation are thus encouraged.

Paisley—Kitchen Educator

Like some but not all participants in this edible schoolyard network, Paisley went to college. In her case, she intended to become a nurse but discovered that dealing with bodily fluids was a "major detriment." She explained:

> I felt like I had the heart for it. I just don't have the stomach for it. I was taking a nutrition class because you have to take one, and the professor that I had was incredible. I realized that . . . the nursing stuff also applies [to] nutrition degree stuff. [The professor] was vegan. She was like some incredible athlete. She did marathons. . . . that was a turning point . . . for me. So, I started to focus more on that aspect. I went to [the community college]. I was taking all my courseloads. I was, like, about ready to transfer. And then, I got really disillusioned. . . . It's harder to get into a program than it is to like get into med school or something like that. So, I dropped out of school and started working in a catering kitchen because they were the only ones who would hire me. I have over 200 cookbooks that I've gone through. I'm learning so I think I'm kind of like an autodidact. I've pretty much taught myself everything that I know in regards to the kitchen. I've taken cooking classes all over the world.

Her interest in the catering business was as much inspired by her interest in cooking as it was by a dislike of the ickiness of nursing:

> I identify as Mexican American; my mom and her family immigrated here in 1988. My grandma was the one who was my caretaker. So, she was always in the kitchen. I mean, she had nine kids. She was always cooking, and I was always in there with her. I was like her 10th child because I was the first of, like, 23 grandchildren. So, my love of cooking and all the things I definitely like . . . I always love[d] to cook, and I always love[d] to eat. . . . I just didn't realize that it would turn into this. I had no idea that, like, I would end up doing this, but I can't imagine myself doing anything else now. And, like, I refer to this place as . . . the Disneyland . . . of a schoolyard, of edible education. Look at our garden, our kitchen across all three sides. It's pretty incredible. Our curriculum, our staff, the support . . . we got everything. And [the local community], I grew up in [there], so my friend sent me the job link,

> and he was like, "Hey, I think you'd be perfect for this." Because I love kids too . . . So, it kind of just went hand in hand. I feel like a big kid myself. So, I think that's why I'm, like, pretty popular on campus, as well. And I think I know that. Me being Mexican, just like they are . . . it plays into, like, representation matters.

Paisley further described what she meant by the kitchen being like Disneyland in describing how the kids would always remember their experiences because "it's not just about cooking. Like, they're cooking together. They're setting up a table together. They're problem-solving: 'This is too salty.' [How] are we going to deal with that? 'Not enough salt.' What are we going to do?"

This brief statement captures the richness of the kitchen experience. Cooking is individual as one needs the sustenance to sustain life. But cooking is also communal, it is social, and it is social in a fundamental manner represented by the setting of the table together. While table-setting, or even what constitutes a table, can vary from culture to culture, the social aspect of dining together is universal in an authentic manner that neat rows of desks in a classroom cannot replicate. Further, the kitchen experience is not just about eating together, but it also involves academics through the necessities of measurements and following recipes at a basic level and at a problem-solving level . . . a higher level. "Your dish is too salty, kiddo, how are you going to solve the problem?" That they are working together makes this a real-world, collaborative, problem-solving opportunity.

Sofia—Kitchen Educator

Sofia, like other edible schoolyard educators, has fond memories of gardening with her family from childhood. Unlike other educators, she approached the edible schoolyard experience later in life:

> Well, I was just, my husband was getting up to, like, "I'm going to be retiring soon." And I decided I needed to get a part-time job. My kids were out of the house. And I was, like, "I'm gonna go to the [school district's] website and see what they have. I'll sign up as a sub after school or whatever" . . . you know, just something to do. And, I saw the farm-to-table kitchen job, and I was, like, "I know exactly what that is" because my husband worked for [a local agricultural company]. And so, I had been to the edible schoolyard . . . at the grand opening and stuff, and I had seen what an awesome place

> that was, and I was, like, "I can do that. I would love it." I didn't know [the school district] had any of that because my kids' school didn't have any of that, you know? So, I applied, and basically, this is how I was raised. You know, growing up, we lived on a quarter of an acre, and half of it was farm for our table, you know? So, we had rabbits for eating and chickens and, you know, goats and stuff and then a garden. And so, I was like, "Okay, I would love to do that. I've taught my kids how to cook. I love to cook." And, you know, they hired me.

Sloane—Kitchen Educator

Sloane had always wanted to be a teacher and recalls role-playing teaching with her friends as a little girl. She did not think she could actually change anyone, but she was hopeful she could be a positive role model for children and have a positive impact in that way. Later, she had kids of her own and worked for a while as a preschool teacher in Colorado before moving to California's Central Valley, where she was a stay-at-home mom. The stay-at-home parenting allowed her to realize that her kids were at school more than they were at home and rekindled her interest in making an impact back in the classroom. Cooking was part of her childhood experience and would also play a role in her re-engaging with schools:

> Something that led me to a teaching career, but I think also with the kitchen . . . I always loved cooking. . . . I can't say, like, "growing up we [had] a farm, and we, you know, [lived] on this," but I spent a lot of my summers in Mexico where my grandma cooks from scratch. She [gets] produce daily, just to get the freshest produce that was around, and I would say the love of cooking started with her. But then, I also took [in] the shows on TV: Julia Child is one of my favorites that I love to watch.

Sloane was living the stay-at-home parent life when efforts began to build a charter school around the edible schoolyard in her rural town:

> And they were petitioning to build [a] school. I attended all those meetings before the start of the school's building. And when I saw what they wanted and what the school was all about, I was all for it. And I thought that was exactly what I wanted for my kids. That's where I want them to go. I just thought it was amazing to make those classroom connections, you know,

> with any laptop because they offer several different electives. We are just one like the many that they have. But I felt like it was going to make my kids roll round it, round and round, get along with life skills. But . . . when I was offered the job, I'm, like, "Oh, what more could I ask for?" These are the two passions of mine. Working with kids, and then on the other hand, getting to do what I love, . . . you know, every day, and that's just cooking, engaging students with food. . . . I believe all students deserve the best education, regardless of where they're from. I was making these strong connections with teachers and having the students make those connections just through the cooking process. And it's, like, when the lightbulb goes off, . . . it's just amazing to see it happen.

Sloane's story stands out in several ways. Despite an early childhood interest in becoming a teacher, it does not appear Sloane pursued a typical teaching career involving college, credentialing, and typical classroom experience. Instead, she found a means to work with her family schedule, such as teaching preschool and then utilizing the time and energy available as a stay-at-home mom to become active as a parent in petitioning for the creation of the edible schoolyard-based charter school in her community. Only after the school opened did she realize that her love of cooking and kids might make her a great match for the kitchen job, which does not necessarily require a teaching credential. Not having the formal training of classroom experience might have even served as a strength for Sloane and other kitchen and garden educators, in that they were open to new innovations in gardening and cooking. Note again, though, the connections with classrooms: Edible schoolyard education is not only about preparing food, but doing so in a manner where "the lightbulb goes off," as students make connections between their experiences with cooking and classroom learning.

Classroom Teachers

Classroom teachers also play a key role in the distributed leadership needed for effective edible schoolyard experiences. Classroom teachers are the regularly credentialed (also called "certified" in some states) teachers hired to lead the regular classroom instruction. In the two charter schools, the classroom teachers can be hired without state teaching credentials, but they are expected to earn them on the job. The teachers here experience what is representative of typical elementary school teaching arrangements: They are assigned to a grade-level team that works together to share responsibility for teaching reading, math, writing, science, and history, according to the state standards, and are accountable to meeting standards assessed through the state standardized tests.

Scarlett—Classroom Teacher

Scarlett grew up in the small town that now features one of the charter schools, a fact she mentioned twice in the interview's first few moments. She loves the community and the kids in the community. Her parents were field workers, and the story of her early life story is worth quoting at some length:

> So, like I mentioned before, I did grow up [here]. . . . My parents were field workers. We didn't have a lot of great advantages growing up. We were so disadvantaged in different ways, whether it was financially, our language barriers . . . both of my parents only speak Spanish, so I was an English learner. So, I definitely wanted to go to school. I didn't want to work in the field like them. I could see how hard it was to go every day from four in the morning 'til five p.m. They would come home exhausted. You know how hot it gets here . . . 110, 115 degrees in the summer. So, I said, like, "I want to do better."

Scarlett did not have access to the garden growing up but did see the toll the field work took on her parents and saw education as means to pursue something "better."

> I went to school to get my BA in criminal justice. And I started doing internships while I was in school. I loved it. But then, I started working for a program at CSUB called College Corps, and that was my first introduction to education. I was a pure, pure college advisor. I would work with high school students just really guiding them in like, "hey, this is what you need to take. Have you registered for your SATs? Are you studying? Are you taking AP classes? Have you met all the A through G requirements?" And I started falling in love with just education and really making the connection with students.

After starting college at the local four-year state university, Scarlett discovered that her goal of "giving back to the community" might be better addressed through education than through criminal justice. She pivoted to education:

> Once students started graduating, they would reach out and just share, like . . . "Thank you so much for this; you really helped me go through this." And that's when I knew this was my calling. So then, I heard about [the charter school]. . . . I decided to apply. I took on an after-school position at that time, and I would come in part-time in the afternoons. And I started off with kinder and first grade and loved the little souls . . . the excitement on their faces. I would work from 3:00 to 6:30 pm, and even then, I was excited to be here for every single thing. The community was amazing. The staff were amazing. Everybody was supportive. So, I said, "okay, I think that this is my calling." And I then started my own family. And I really liked the time schedule for myself as well. And then our principal back in the day decided, "hey, like, why don't you go back to school? You're meant to do this. You talk about how much you love it. You know, we're offering a program that allows you to go to school and still work." So, I said, "all right, I'm gonna do it." And I went back to school. I got my credential and my master's in teaching, and now, I'm here, and honestly, it's the best decision that I've made. The kids are so loving. They are humble. I would say that that is the biggest thing about our students here. They are so thankful and thoughtful about all the things that we do for them and the families. . . . "Thank you so much for what you do for my kids. Thank you. Thank you. Thank you." And it reminds me so much of my parents being thankful [for educators]. . . . I know that they are not able to give their [children] all their resources and all the things they need. I can see how thankful they are for it. So that's how I got [into] education.

Scarlett is in many ways similar to Jose, who grew up in the community with field-working parents and found education as a way out of the hardship and poverty of the immigrant fieldworker experience—in other words, seizing the opportunities America has to offer. In doing so, however, the pull of community remained strong and she, like Jose, intentionally returned to the small community to serve as a model and a guide for future students. Notably, she did not just return to a regular school with an emphasis solely on the mechanical requirements of standardized testing. Rather, she returned to a school with a garden and kitchen emphasis, recognizing the relevance these facilities and experiences can play in both academics and in the community and social life of the students. She and Jose both recognize the value of these garden and kitchen experiences. The academic focus of the school and the utilization of the gardens and kitchens are an experience toward the end of learning what might be considered more traditional measures of academic achievement.

This emphasis is implicitly expressed in Scarlett's own experience when she discusses the "supportive environment" offered at the school. She could have been encouraged to stay as a picker or field worker but on a smaller scale in the school garden. But that is not what happened. Instead, she was encouraged to return to school to obtain her teaching credential and master's degree to bring solid academics to the classroom that would connect with the garden and kitchen experiences. Further, Scarlett's own perceptions are supported by the community buzz created when the school was first proposed, and the present-day family and community support for the school, as parents recognize that the gardens and kitchens provide opportunities for learning that are not available at other schools.

Jasper—Classroom Teacher

Jasper grew up in the United States but spent summers in Mexico. Her grandfather was a field worker and her dad was a truck driver moving produce, fruits, and vegetables to the market. She is a native of the community and so was surrounded by the fields and migrant workers. She recognized that education was a key pathway out of the fields, and so she attended California State University, Monterey Bay, where she pursued a degree in liberal studies. She also tutored migrant workers in English in the Salinas area before returning to family. She explains her commitment to education:

> I feel like education is very important, and it even starts with where you eat from, right? We didn't have a lot. . . . I always thought it was fascinating that we lived around fields here, but we didn't have that much access to [what was in them]. I remember mom saying that groceries were a little bit more pricey, you know. You would think because we're surrounded by fields. . . . So, I feel that whenever I started tutoring the kids, I really enjoyed . . . teaching them to read. So, . . . my background is really reading education with that, as well. So, I think it all goes together.

As communicated by multiple educators involved with gardens and kitchens from a Hispanic background, the garden and kitchen experiences are not seen as supplanting the traditional academic skills—reading, writing, and math—that promise better opportunity in the United States, but instead supplementing these skills. The question is not, "gardens or academics," but rather a commitment to "gardens *and* academics." Jasper explains the importance of eating right and laments the lack of access to affordable, healthy food even in the midst of industrial scale agriculture. But she moves on to the tutoring and teaching to read, which suggests the promise of more.

Jasper's interest in the Edible School Yard program specifically was inspired by her younger sister's experience at one of the rural charter schools. In Jasper's own words:

> My sister came to school here. She started third grade. She's graduating today, actually, from [the local high school]. When I was living in Monterey, she would talk about the school a lot, and we moved her from another school. . . . [T]he only thing she would share was about the ESY. So, she would say, "I got to go to the kitchen today. I got to go to the garden today." And I'm, like, "They have a garden at your school?" She's, like, "Yeah, it's right in the middle. Everything's there, and we get to go." She was fascinated by actually being able to touch and . . . actually do activities. Then she would bring recipes home and expose my mom to new foods. And so my mom would then cook for us when I would come home for the summer. My sister kept all her recipes. And so, I'm, like, my little sister . . . I mean, she's a third grader. . . . She started halfway [through] third grade here. She had never really shown an interest in school. And when I graduated, a couple of my friends had already worked here. And I asked, . . . "[W]hat do you think I could apply . . . for?" (I hadn't finished my teaching yet.) I go, and my little sister's really happy with it as well, and I feel like that's really important. . . . I went to the [local] schools, and they . . . didn't have any of that, you know, and so I said, "You know what? I'm going to try it because I feel like it gives . . . a good mix with education because your mental health has a lot to do with the way you eat or what you're exposed to." Especially because I feel like it gave the kids value, especially their parents or farmworkers, because they get to actually go out there and grow things . . . and see their fruits and vegetables growing . . . And then being able to cook them in the kitchen . . . So, I was more intrigued [about] why my sister was so happy with it.

Note again the consistency with the themes we have seen from others. There is an emphasis on academics: Jasper's sister is graduating from high school on the day of the interview. This is not "garden education *or* academics," it is gardens *for* academics, which is putting into practice the model Dewey suggested of connecting the classroom and the garden. We also see the student engagement and excitement about the garden experiences, especially through the "touch," and actually doing activities. There is also another example of the connection with the families, as Jasper's sister would bring the kitchen's recipes home, and her mom would cook them, thus "exposing my mom to new foods." The key line in here though is, "She [the sister] had never really shown an interest for school." With the gardens providing a tactile environment that clearly appealed to her learning style and desire for authentic experiences, such as cooking new foods she could share with her mom, the gardens and kitchens became a pathway to greater education and not the disappointing recreation of field work some critics have suggested.

School Level Administration and Academic Coaches

School principals and assistant principals bear the primary responsibility for setting the vision of the school and providing administrative support through securing funding, arranging scheduling, determining curriculum, developing instruction, and supporting the school vision through other tasks. While principals are the primary instructional leaders in their schools, assistant principals and academic coaches provide evaluation of and support in instructional techniques.

Layla—Academic Coach

Layla started out as an accountant in undergraduate work but discovered there was no "joy" in the profession. Her dad had been an accountant, and so believed that should be the way to go. However, her mother had been a teacher, so she switched to education. She shared, "[I am] very passionate about education because I 100% believe in its power to change." Note the social justice implications here, the belief that schools can make things better. This belief is reiterated in her later emphasis on the importance of graduation: "I just went to, . . . as a matter of fact, I went to three graduation parties last weekend. So, my last class before becoming a coach, those students are graduating from high school. . . . I don't even know how to describe in words [what it is like] to be at those parties and interact with my students who were once fifth graders and see what they're on the path to becoming." Note the emphasis on academics here (the graduation), along with community (the parties), and the implicit joy involved. This is not the garden or academics but rather the garden *and* academics.

This theme of gardens and academics finds further substance in Layla's visit to the Edible Schoolyard at Berkeley, which provided a good picture of what this could be. "It wasn't just kids going there and learning things and learning how to garden and learning about organic food. . . . But it was also that the . . . garden was very intertwined with the school." The themes of health and community reemerged at this point, as the Berkeley garden was originally a parking lot, and kids were bringing "yucky" food to eat at school. The gardens provided an opportunity for a new vision for health, and in the process, "that extension of the classroom into something very real world and very hands on."

The impact on the health of kids and even the community can be seen in Layla's own kids: "By far, of my three sons, the least picky eater was the youngest who had access to this garden and kitchen." She further elaborates, "He is much more open if you put something weird that looks strange in front of him. He'll try it, you know, and then he'll tell you it's not his favorite." Her youngest will even eat kimchi.

Zoe—Assistant Principal

Once again, the influence of positive memories growing up has influenced interest in the gardens as an adult. In this case, Zoe grew up in the farming community of Watsonville in Central California and near Santa Cruz, a major surfing capital of the United States. Watsonville is home to several well-known agricultural brands, including Driscoll's, known for their strawberries, and Martinelli's, known for apples and especially their sparkling apple juice. Growing up, Zoe recounts, "I always tease my dad that he was a hippie before it was cool. And so, it really came from my family. First of all, my parents have always really grown their own garden and made it not just a place where you eat but also a refuge of sorts." As happens with aging and responsibility, including the responsibility of raising triplets, the time and energy needed to grow her own garden made the process difficult for Zoe to carry forward at her own home. When [the charter school] opened, she was intrigued.

> When the school opened, knowing that one of the centerpieces of the school was the kitchen and garden, it was just really impactful because I wanted to

> make sure my kids also didn't just hear from me about health and wellness, but that it's a way of life and . . . it requires a lifetime of making choices that are healthy.

The school, then, offered a unique and welcomed opportunity to reignite her interest in the ground and growing while simultaneously supporting a healthier lifestyle for her kids.

Back home, Zoe describes the community as one where "a lot of families work in the fields," and "they're out there, they're working hard in the sun, but then that food really doesn't go to them. It goes to many other people." The supermarket in the community mostly sold processed foods, and the little bit of produce offered was of poor quality. She shares how her neighbor had cherries that were beautiful and fresh, probably purchased in nearby Bakersfield, but the cherries available in the local store were bruised. Yet, by having this conversation along with others in the community, and having the same conversation with the store manager, the quality and quantity of available produce changed. The school will introduce a new recipe, and families go looking for the ingredients, creating a new demand. In the process, fresher food becomes available, and families develop advocacy skills resulting in a healthier, fresher community store.

Yet the gardens are not just about eating well. There are intentional connections to academics, specifically, developing a college-going culture. Zoe recounts, regarding her own kids, "I knew that my kids would go to college," and that attitude toward her own kids infused her approach to the garden education. Regarding her daughter's experience,

> I feel that I'm kind of coming full circle because my, my daughter, who started here as a second grader, just graduated from high school, and . . . she made us a casserole, and she goes, "I'm so sorry, mom. I didn't use all the most healthy ingredients, but it's homemade." So, it's just those things, knowing that she's gonna go off to college, but she knows . . . what is healthy.

Luca—Principal

Luca started the year as assistant principal and moved into the principalship upon the principal's spring resignation. She was previously at the school about nine months (July to April) before becoming principal, so she is very new. The transition is typical of her working her way up the ladder, starting as a substitute, then teacher intern, teacher (kindergarten, first, second, fifth), then intervention specialist, then academic coach, assistant principal, and principal. She is a first-generation college graduate.

Regarding experiences that drew her to teaching, Luca recalls a teacher she had, and the explanation is worth quoting at length:

> As a student, I had [names her favorite teacher]. I don't know if you know her, but she's with the [names school district]. She was my junior high language arts teacher, and I think she was one of the first people to push the rigor with me. . . . I had just gone through school. It was easy for me, . . . and I just . . . did the work. You know how, if you're a great student, sometimes it is easy, and at that moment, it wasn't easy. But she saw . . . my aptitude and challenged me, and I . . . remember a lot of writing projects, research projects, that I had done in her class that . . . really just inspired me, thinking, like, well, I'm able to do more. I think that's when the lightbulb went off specifically for me: "I can do whatever I want. I can do it." I'm the first to graduate college in my family.

Notice the emphasis on rigor. The rigor of being "challenged" through writing and research projects really inspired Luca and built her confidence to the point of being the first in her family to graduate from college. This formative experience is now being brought to the garden with intentionality to make the garden and kitchen the same sort of inspiring project, leading to classroom success as she had. Luca continues, regarding the importance of experiences in cultivating classroom rigor with:

> I think that, and then, it's just a non-traditional education, but my family did travel a lot as a child, and I feel like I learned through experiencing national parks and museums and all of that. I feel like that really, really helped me connect in the classroom, like in reflection. Without those opportunities, I don't think I would have been successful in understanding and having a really good worldview.

For Luca, the gardens and kitchen form a variation on the essential experiences that inform and support the classroom instruction, which for her were national parks and museums, but for her students are the gardens and kitchens. Again, this is representative of Dewey who saw the gardens and kitchens (well gardens back in his day) as connected to the classroom, not just a stand-alone free-for-all type activity.

Hayden—Principal

Like Luca, Hayden's educational journey started as a substitute teacher. However, his experience began in urban Los Angeles, Inglewood to be exact. Reflecting on the experience, Hayden reminisces, "Some said try substituting, it's an easy gig. They weren't honest." Taking the subbing gig as temporary employment:

> I quickly realized that the stereotypes of what was explained to me were true of the inner city. Expectations were lowered. The rigor, all components were less than, and so I immediately tried to raise the standard so much so that at the end of my first day as a day-to-day substitute, they had a full year contract for me waiting at the end of the day.

He continues to elaborate on "heart-wrenching" stories in the traditional school setting, such as students asking to attend his class because their regular teacher was asleep and then going to the other teacher's classroom and smelling "the air of alcohol."

From the beginning then, Hayden's interest was in raising student achievement, bringing in academic success through rigor, and he was working in a particularly challenging inner-city environment. As time progressed, he became interested in the charter school movement as means to further his interest in promoting academic rigor:

> [I was] hearing quite a bit about charter schools, the charter system, and . . . I knew that I was in . . . it was in alignment with my goals and values, in the sense that, to be honest, they advertise it as merit-based pay. "We're going to reward those who are meeting standards and producing outcomes, meeting the standards." And then as I got into it, I just bought into the schools of choice. . . . I then joined ISEF, Inner City Educational Foundation. And [I] began as an instructor, then slowly but surely, I made my way into administration.

Even in this inner-city environment, the interest in rigor expanded into an interest in projects and real-world experiential learning. In an early administrative gig, Hayden became principal of a charter high school in inner-city

Los Angeles where there was no cafeteria, lunch was contracted out, and students ate at picnic tables in a dirt lot. He did have access to some petty cash from textbook sales, and he took some of that cash to Home Depot and bought a tarp and some bricks and other supplies to build simple planters in the parking lot.

True to his interest in establishing rigor, and coincidentally true to Dewey's vision of connecting garden and classroom experiences, he then turned his attention to getting the science department to utilize the space. He noted that "the kids gravitated to it," suggesting the authentic engagement that experiential garden learning brings. It also demonstrates that the gardens promote an asset-based form of learning rather than a deficit form.

Not all connections with the classroom are based on academic progress. Sometimes, the more basic elements of nutrition come into play. Again, recalling an experience in South Los Angeles, Hayden recalls the food insecurity of the area:

> So, I think it was, again, working in the inner city and seeing what was provided to students for nutrition, what the students thought was nutritious, but through no fault of their own. It was all they could afford. It was, you know, looking at a parent buying just bags of Top Ramen, or I remember a student arriving at school with a suitcase. He was out playing a little late, and I [asked], "What is he still doing here?" "[H]e came to school today and said his mom kicked him out of the house. And he doesn't have anywhere to go." . . . I went to the home, and the reason [his mom] kicked him out was because he had a single mom [with] varying ages of [children]. He had . . . it was food he had eaten, too much food. And he does not understand that it has to be shared with the whole family. And I'll never forget, she said that he opened up a bottle of Prego, made a meal for himself, and then put the bottle of Prego back in the cabinet. So, she, as a mom, thought she had a meal ready for her kids, and she didn't.

Even when food is available, the nutritional value may not be that great in high-poverty areas: "So, kids would get on the city bus as early as 4:30 am from Watts to travel to my high school. And, and in that time, what they had for breakfast were nacho chips." Seeing the kids eating nacho chips for an early morning breakfast provided the "aha moment" regarding connections among nutrition, energy, engagement, and even class management:

> And I just found myself constantly [saying], "Hey, why don't you eat this? Why don't you eat that?" And just seeing, you know, what a difference it made—energy, you know—and then try[ing] also to get individuals to realize the relationship between nutrients and behavior and classroom management . . . and you know, you can't focus if you're hungry. You can't focus if your body's having difficulty digesting something.

This, in turn, led to the establishment of a garden, again in an inner-city environment where the garden started as a tarp with some dirt held in by bricks in the parking lot:

> And so that's what first put it in my mind. We were trying to build out some of the electives we offered our high school students. And I said, "It'd be nice if we get culinary, you know. . . . What if they take this garden and produce x, y, or z?" And so when I arrived here to find out that, no, it's just a school such as this, that realizes that this is the original project-based learning . . . it reminded me of my childhood and how you make authentic discoveries, you know, just by running in a field in Bakersfield. . . . It allows students to do it, hear it, and then finally students take ownership of what's been produced.

Indeed, there is something to say, "What a difference . . . not only having green grass and trees, but seeing something grow and develop and then reaping its rewards."

And the rewards are not just for the kids. Again emphasizing the food desert aspect of inner city life, Hayden shared, "I was, like, where, where's the produce going? And come to find out the adults are taking it because they are hungry and realized that they couldn't provide anything for their kids." Hayden describes a letter written by a student in this rural edible schoolyard school:

> One of the most passionate letters that a student ever wrote was to the PE teacher, to the garden teacher, and the kitchen teacher, talking about . . . how much they'll never forget [that] they changed their life, . . . opening up about [how learning about] . . . the benefits of raw fruits and vegetables had a direct line with their weight. They used to be bullied about being out of shape, and because of [the three teachers], they now are doing this.

This is from a kid who used to eat Takis and was introduced to fresh, whole, raw foods through the garden. Apricots specifically were mentioned. The commentary on freshness continues, as Hayden noted that it was not good role modeling for staff to be running to McDonald's at lunch and having to "hide the bag on the way back." So instead, he introduced a competition among staff to eat healthier themselves, and they discovered, "you know, if you make a salad just right, it can be quite filling." Practice what you preach and create equity with staff and students.

Executive Level Leadership

While our network of schools encompasses two large elementary school districts and one charter school network, the edible schoolyards themselves are supported by a common educational foundation dedicated to growing the edible schoolyard movement. The foundation provides support through curriculum development, professional development for all educators involved in the network, assisting in securing grant funding, and providing strategic vision. In other words, the foundation provides support specific to the edible schoolyards that one might generally expect to find from superintendents and their assistant superintendents of academics, finance, and facilities in a typical larger school district.

Diego—Program Director

Diego grew up in a household where his mom worked as a first-grade teacher. Education was therefore important, but he "never had an interest in going into education." Instead, he worked several odd jobs, most of them involving manual outdoor labor. Diego's pride in his ability to work hard, or as he puts it, his "grit," clearly shines forth. His transition to becoming a curriculum developer and community relations person for the Grimm Family Educational Foundation was, "happenstance." He had no "idea what the weird garden was." He did have an interest in the seed-to-table cycles. Growing up in Bakersfield, his home did have a garden that included chickens. He has fond memories of "grandma working in her garden," where he experienced and grew fascinated with the cycles that lead to seeds producing food for the table. Specifically, he recalls from the age of five making zucchini bread with the zucchini his grandma harvested from the garden, "I can still smell it and see it hanging out around her counter."

A little while later while a senior in high school, while other kids were spending their money on movies and whatnot, Diego invested $20 he had into baby chicks, which he raised for garden fresh eggs for his house. Further, he indulged his fascination with the seed-to-table cycle by buying and raising his own seeds. While other kids looked through toy catalogs, he instead remembers reading seed catalogs.

These childhood memories of gardening with grandma have been seen before. In the decision to start a garden at school, one might be well advised to consider if gardening is part of the community fabric already, as it certainly is in the agriculturally-rich San Joaquin Valley. Having a community interest in gardening already might pave the path for school gardens; otherwise, perhaps consider pursuing other avenues of engaging learning that more closely fit the community interests and strengths. Or, pursue the garden anyway as a novel idea and one that promises to connect students more closely with their natural environment, as Dewey envisioned. So, when the opportunity to work in the "weird garden" came up, Diego thought:

> Oh, this is awesome. I can pair getting to work outside, working outdoors pushing myself in that sort of way, with this really cool teaching component to see the life cycles. So, where I was getting at with that is that . . . there's the best of both worlds for me because . . . I could work outside and have fun working in the dirt, and then also getting to help support a great cause.

The great cause finds form in the garden and the kitchen experiences but really boils down to helping "the next generation of citizens in our community be better in health and wellness." Notice here the gardens and kitchens are not ends in and of themselves but rather means to the ends of a broader vision of citizenship, community, health, and wellness—again, Dewey's vision encapsulated in the connections with environment, school, and community. Notice also that the garden experiences capture Dewey's vision by building on what the kids are interested in. These stories of fond memories of gardens in their youth are examples of engaging learning based on personal experiences.

The actual transition to the garden employment was by "happenstance," as Diego's girlfriend at the time already worked with the gardens and suggested he apply as "an extra in the garden." Despite this "accident,"

Diego quickly became inspired by the garden work and particularly the opportunity to teach students "creatively." The job combined his passion for outdoor manual labor and his fascination with the seed-to-table cycle into one job that also promised to engage new learners.

Rowan—President, Educational Foundation

Rowan wastes little time in communicating his, and the foundation's, vision for edible schoolyards: "The original model was really about blending education, high achievement, and college-bound dynamics in rural communities and partnering that with a wellness program and edible schoolyard program."

The top leadership establishes a vision wherein the gardens are not simply for flowers at the expense of learning math, but instead, it is a blended or integrated approach to strong academics leading to college, along with wellness, and implemented through an engaging school yard program. By default or design, this integration of overall wellness, community, and academic rigor implements Dewey's vision in the 21st century. The Grimm Family Foundation's actual vision states: "To expand education and wellness across Kern County so that all will thrive and be successful in school and in life and to promote and support the Grow Public Schools' mission to offer a choice in educational opportunities" (Grimm Family Foundation, 2018).

And the Grimm Family Foundation's mission states:

> Helping make vibrant communities in Kern County with our charter schools and Edible Schoolyard programs by closing the achievement gap, improving the health of students and families, and creating economic growth in the communities that we serve. By being fiscally responsible and innovative, we will broaden community impact through our programs, partnerships, research, fund development, and community outreach. (Grimm Family Foundation, 2018).

Note the emphasis on words indicative of an emphasis on academic rigor, "education," "successful in school," "closing the achievement gap," and even "creating economic opportunities." Consistent with Dewey, however, the mission and vision also emphasize the whole child as a citizen within a community through phrases such as "vibrant communities," "community impact," and "wellness."

Consistent with the foundation's emphasis on local community, Rowan emphasizes they are looking to build 200 points of light, very deeply in one county. Indeed, rather than being stars in the sky, Rowan is committed to growing deep roots (pun intended).

Rowan brings organizational consultation and strategic planning to the garden movement. The consulting business he founded was hired by Barbara Grimm of the Grimm Family Educational Foundation to provide a strategic plan for the schools and the foundation. Rowan does have connections to education, primarily through consulting with diverse higher education institutions. Rowan serves a leadership and administrative role in recognizing the need for the foundation and the schools to have a firm financial footing and strategic plan to start small and grow larger (but not too large, as they want to focus on the local community).

Upon establishing the first two schools, they moved to focusing on community events such as using mobile kitchens and looking to expand community partnerships. When COVID-19 hit, they still promoted community through turning the gardens into "mini farms" from which they could address food insecurity, through such means as supporting the local food banks. With the end of COVID-19, they are reverting to a stronger focus on education and the role gardens and kitchens can play in education.

Summarizing Thoughts

Rowan articulates and promotes a strong vision for what edible schoolyard education can be in serving students and their communities, and that vision permeates the edible schoolyard movement in the Southern San Joaquin Valley. The edible schoolyards are at once a place where students can literally get their hands dirty planting, cultivating, and harvesting food they will later work with their peers to turn into nutritious and delicious meals. In doing so, they engage in authentic learning with real-world applications to the basics of a healthy lifestyle. Simultaneously, there is a strong emphasis on academics and connections among the gardens, kitchens, and regular classrooms. The participants regularly talked about the importance of school and the opportunity for future learning, such as college.

Further, the edible schoolyard experience promotes an inclusive education. The several schoolyard roles examined include a diversity of participant-educators with a range of backgrounds. Some started in education from deeply rooted childhood interests in always wanting to be a teacher. Others arrived at the edible schoolyards as seniors, even as a retirement gig. Some brought formal instructional training represented by teacher credentialing; others arrived at the edible schoolyards through life's inevitable twists and turns, leaving careers in business and other fields to engage students in learning experiences they wish they had had themselves. The participants also represent a diversity of ethnic and national backgrounds: white, Black, Hispanic, Mexican, and Filipino. A surprising number are immigrants themselves or are first generation Americans having been born here to immigrant parents.

The immigrant experience provides one of the most interesting findings in this study, as it addresses one of the criticisms leveled against garden education. Flanagan (2010) supposes a hypothetical Mexican immigrant who makes the illegal and dangerous journey to the United States and finds labor picking lettuce, peppers, and grapes in the fields under the hot sun. But he made this journey to embrace the promise of America, to provide a better opportunity for his kids. Yet, when he enrolls them in their local garden-based school, he finds they are not learning reading, writing, and math but instead are out in the hot sun growing and picking lettuce, peppers, and grapes.

The immigrant experiences in our study do not represent this hypothetical critique, first and foremost in that the edible schoolyards here pursue connections with academic learning with intentionality, as will be explored in more detail in Chapters 6 and 7. But the experiences reported in our study schools move beyond academics to creating welcoming environments, exactly the types of environments parents want, and in which students best learn. Indeed, a number of our educator-participants, regardless of immigrant status, chose to send their own children to these schools for exactly this reason. One participant actively promoted the school's creation in her community so her children could go there long before she was employed by the school. Participant-educators, especially immigrant participants, but those also representing the spectrum of educators, consistently referred to fond memories of gardening and cooking with their parents, grandparents, tias (aunts), and tios (uncles) in the United States and in Mexico. These are fond memories, and the gardens and kitchens are seen as places where these memories are recreated for the next generation. In other words, the school gardens and kitchens provide environments in which students are already familiar and work to promote an interest in school by providing a familiar, welcoming, and interesting place. The edible schoolyard, therefore, serves as a gateway toward academics and socialization, goals of which Dewey would approve.

References

Bass, B. M., Avolio, B. J., & Atwater, L. (1996). The transformational and transactional leadership of men and women. *Applied Psychology: An International Review, 45*(1), 5–34.

Canterino, F., Cirella, S., Piccoli, B., & Shani, A. B. (2020). Leadership and change mobilization: The mediating role of distributed leadership. *Journal of Business Research, 108*, 42–51. https://doi.org/10.1016/j.jbusres.2019.09.052

Dewey, J. (2010). *The school and society and the child and the curriculum* (2nd ed.). Digireads.com publishing. (Original work published 1915).

Dewey, J. (2016). *Democracy and education.* Ozymandias Press. (Original work published 1916).

Dewey, J., & Dewey, E. (1962). *Schools of tomorrow*. E. P. Dutton & Co., Inc. (Original work published 1915).

Grimm Family Education Foundation. (2018). *Home*. https://www.grimmeducation.org/

English, F. W. (2002). The penetration of educational leadership texts by revelation and prophecy: The case of Stephen R. Covey. *Journal of School Leadership, 12*(1), 4–22. https://doi-org.csub.idm.oclc.org/10.1177/105268460201200101

Flanagan, C. (2010, January/February). Cultivating failure: How school gardens are cheating our most vulnerable population. *The Atlantic*, 101–111.

Hallinger, P. (2003). Leading educational change: Reflections on the practice of instructional and transformational leadership. *Cambridge Journal of Education, 33*(3), 329–351. https://doi.org/10.1080/0305764032000122005

Harris, A., & DeFlammis, J. (2016). Distributed leadership in practice: Evidence, misconceptions and possibilities. *Management in Education, 30*(4), 141–146. https://doi.org/10.1177/089 2020616656734

Harris, A., Leithwood, K., Day, C., Sammons, P., & Hopkins, D. (2007). Distributed leadership and organizational change: Reviewing the evidence. *Journal of Educational Change, 8*, 337–347. https://doi.org/10.1007/s10833-007-9048-4

Knoll, M. (2022). *Beyond rhetoric: New perspectives on John Dewey's pedagogy*. International Academic Publishers.

Leithwood, K., & Jantzi, D. (2005). A review of transformational school leadership research 1996–2005. *Leadership and Policy in Schools, 4*, 177–199. https://doi.org/10.1080/15700760500244769

Liu, Y., Sukru Bellibas, M., & Gumus, S. (2021). The effect of instructional leadership and distributed leadership on teacher self-efficacy and job satisfaction: Mediating roles of supportive school culture and teacher collaboration. *Education Management Administration & Leadership, 49*(3), 430–453. https://doi.org/10.1177/1741143220910438

Moolenaar, N. M., Daly, A. J., & Sleegers, P. J. C. (2010). Occupying the principal position: Examining relationships between transformational leadership, social network position, and schools' innovative climate. *Educational Administration Quarterly, 46*(5), 623–670.

Ylimaki, R. M. (2012). Curriculum leadership in a conservative era. *Educational Administration Quarterly, 48*(2), 304–346. https://doi.org/10.1177/0013161X11427393 https://doi.org/ 10.1177/0013161X10378689

CHAPTER SIX

FAVORITE PROJECTS FOR LEARNING

The Edible Schoolyard provides hands-on learning and sensory experience to students through garden and kitchen classrooms. Our goal is to help every child fall in love with fresh, seasonal produce.

The Edible Schoolyard Kern County

How does one go about fulfilling the vision, mission, and promise of edible schoolyard education? John Dewey himself faced many challenges in actually implementing his visionary ideas in a real school with real students (Knoll, 2022), although he and Evelyn Dewey (1915/1962) documented several schools from a century ago that had more success in implementing experience-based, authentic, engaging learning. This learning even included both gardens and kitchens, among other experiences. To find out what happens in the gardens and kitchens, I observed lessons of each, along with asking educators at all levels to share their favorite lessons. Because children and teachers alike are diverse, and because things do not always go according to plan, I also sought to find out what happens in those times when an unexpected turn of events might occur, such as an unexpected event or disruption that might lead to an "aha!" type learning moment. The educators shared a variety of such moments and other favorite lessons that can be summarized into three categories: individual insights, structure versus flexibility, and community-building. These findings roughly parallel the self-determination theory goals, essentially a more detailed and modernized version of Dewey's vision, of competence, autonomy, and relatedness. Here are their stories.

Competence

Learning is never complete, and indeed it probably did not happen at all, unless the student is more competent in knowledge or skills, or both, following the lesson than they were before. Self-determination theory emphasizes that competence revolves around feelings of operating effectively within one's important life contexts. Perhaps no lesson more fascinatingly illustrated this education principle than the kitchens' use of knives. These are real knives, not toys, and the students from the earliest ages, that is, first grade, are using these actual kitchen tools to cut the food they are preparing to eat, although some accommodation is made for what type of real knife is used at what age. As kitchen educator Sofia shared:

> I will say that my favorite experience with the kids is the first time they get to use real knives. We started off with little plastic cutters. And you know, then we introduce them to real knives, and the kids are like, you know, "Are [we] going to be okay . . .?" It's, like, "Of course, because we have rules. We have expectations that are nice safety things, and if you follow them forever, you're not gonna lose a finger." And then after they've used the knives a couple of times, they, you know, . . . you better not give them a plastic cutter again because they're, like, "I'm a knife expert. Why would we ever go backward?" So, I guess, seeing them, like, . . . you have trust in them. . . . It's like, you know, "you've done a good job, we trust that you're gonna be good, you know, be able to . . . handle it and everything." . . . And so that back-and-forth with them I think is probably my favorite experience.

The plastic cutters referred to here are still knives but are plastic with a corrugated edge and are still appropriate for cutting softer fruits and vegetables. The real knives presented are actual chef's knives with safety protocols, including proper holding of the knives and forming a "claw" with your other hand to hold the object being cut, which greatly reduces the chance of slicing a finger. For a visual representation, simply watch any cooking show on TV, which also points to the lesson's relevance. When finished with the knife, it is to be placed on the back edge of the cutting board, sharp edge facing away from the user—not a bad idea to implement at home.

Radishes formed a surprisingly common favorite food experience, especially because even some of the teachers themselves do not particularly care for radishes. Incidentally, no one is allowed to say, "I don't like it," when trying any of the food in the edible schoolyard. Instead, students must at least taste everything they prepared, and if they actually do not like it, they are then allowed to say, "not my favorite," and pass on eating more. Honestly, as the author and a parent, I wish I had used this technique when my own kids were little. In reality, students in the kitchens rarely do not like the foods they are trying, possibly because they literally grew at least some of the ingredients and certainly prepared the dishes themselves. They are invested in a quality product and determined to enjoy the fruits of their labor. This brings us back to radishes and this story from Lydia, a program specialist at the urban school:

> We'd just started our garden. We're having our very first harvest, and what grows fastest is radish. So, we're doing our radish harvest, and we know we want to have a radish tasting in the garden. . . . So, we decided to do an official tasting, and we created a radish . . . recipe that the students would be able to assemble themselves [and order]. So, we went all out. . . . We put linens on our table, music, and each got their individual setup, create their own order, which included fresh radish . . . among other things, and we're out there doing it, and the kids are all excited, and we have this little student named Jacob. . . . He's a first grader at this time. He has spent his whole life only eating chicken nuggets and macaroni and cheese. So, Jacob is here with this radishy thing, but he's adamant he's not eating. "Not my favorite. . . ." They've got this smear of Greek yogurt, and . . . lemon, and the Himalayan salt . . . the whole thing. And he's doing it, but he's, like, "I'm not eating this." Like kids around him are building theirs, and they start eating [theirs]. And they're, like, "Oh my gosh, this is so good." And they're . . . still doing well. "Why don't you just look at them?" "Oh, okay." So, he picks one up, and he closes his eyes and takes a bite and then blinks his eyes open, and he's, like, "this is good" and chews it up. [He eats his second one], and immediately he starts looking around the table for who hasn't finished their second one. . . . He loves it. This changed his life because from that day, he started trying new foods. I worked with his parents; they were here every day picking him up. And he would try grapes and then he tried apples and then he tried greens and then he tried broccoli, but he just absolutely expanded his whole horizon and food-tasting because of that one lesson in the garden with the radish.

Jacob's story, as shared by Lydia, was not the only viewpoint of the value of radishes. Damien, another program specialist at the same urban school, shared:

> They want to learn, and they want you to have standards. They want you to teach them . . . like every other child. Like, I come in here and treat this like a private school. I do everything that a private school would do. I don't ever make any choices [where I wouldn't] want to do [the same] for my kids. This is not what these kids get. And then the second lesson was my first introduction to teaching them "cycle" because, you know, radishes grow in like 19-28 days or something like that. So, [we] planted radishes, and what do you eat? I mean, "come on, man, the radishes," so what do you do? Well, we had an order party, and . . . it was awesome. And I decorated underneath here, and it looked like [a local favorite restaurant]. . . . We had jazz music . . . and I had like these little light streams. So, they walked through, and it was . . . so fun. And I told them this is an hors d'oeuvres party. So, . . . they made little radishes with Triscuits, radishes, lemon, and yogurt. Oh, and salt, real sea salt.

Damien's viewpoint of this story further emphasizes the connections between radishes and competence in learning. While Jacob learned to try and like new things, a form of competence in and of itself readily observable to anyone who has raised their own kids, Damien's version emphasizes the radishes' usefulness in teaching the academic concept of the lifecycle. Notably, the radish takes only about 28 days to grow from a seed to being served on a cracker with lemon, yogurt, and a touch of sea salt, thus making the radish an ideal vegetable to grow in a time-constrained school setting.

While the competence of learning life cycles through the radish's seed-to-table journey is emphasized here, it is also worth noting the dining experience that built social skills, as Dewey would say, or relatedness, as self-determination theory might address. Here, Damien and the other teachers had the students prepare the radishes into fancy and tasty hors-d'oeuvres, which were served at tables covered in cloths with jazz music playing in the background. They recreated the ambiance of a popular community restaurant and enjoyed good food and one another's company. Talk about creating a welcoming environment!

Radishes are not the only means to teach the seed-to-table cycle. When asked about his favorite lesson, Diego, a program director at the edible schoolyard, unhesitatingly replies:

> The big one that always comes to mind is probably the plant parts. Really, I get to see both ends of it. So, I'm going to talk about both ends of it, you

> know, on the garden side and the kitchen side because there are lessons and benefits on both ends. We also do plant parts and plant anatomy lessons in the garden. I think it's in, like, second grade. It might even be as soon as first grade. But we're going over the basic parts of a plant. So, [we're] talking about the roots, the stems, the leaves, and the flower, and then the seeds and how that reproduction system occurs . . . not necessarily going into pollination but talking about the parts of the plant. . . . And you can use a sunflower, so it's a great way to be able to teach the plant lesson, but then what's really awesome, and this is where I talk about closure . . . the entire seed-to-table cycle. . . . And then we have the plant parts salad which is in the kitchen, and the plant part of the salad is really neat because it uses every single part of a plant whether it's one plant, but typically it's multiple [plants]. . . . [Y]ou use a root . . . you use a carrot . . . radish . . . and then you use the stem. You can use chard stems in a salad; you typically don't want kale stems, but there are a lot of different vegetables where you can utilize the stem in a recipe, and then you go to the leaf. So many leaves, . . . leafy greens, are used in a salad. And then you can go to the flower. Lots of flowers are used [as] edible flowers . . . in salads. And then you go to the seed. We love putting sunflower seeds in our salads and mixing those together. So, you get to see it on both ends. We can show the students how there are parts of a plant, and they're all there in order for a plant to survive, and each one has its own benefit . . . benefit to the plant. And then you bring it on this end, and you show [that] each one of the benefits to the plant also has a benefit to the body.

Again, the garden and the kitchen are much more than simply growing flowers at the expense of mathematics. Scientific concepts appropriate to the grade level are much more than taught, they are experienced by students as they plant, tend to, harvest, and finally eat the quite literal fruits (and vegetables) of their labor. Notice the emphasis Diego places on the grade-level appropriateness. The seed-to-table cycle is appropriate for the first or second grade. Diego even wryly notes that they do not necessarily go over the pollination part of the cycle at this young age, which is probably a good call to avoid potentially awkward conversations in the first grade classroom.

Corn also plays a significant role in the edible schoolyards. The rather large kernel size of corn can be used in lessons about the parts of seeds, as students dissect corn kernels, preferably utilizing their previously learned knife skills as Damien implies:

> I have to probably go back to my first lesson after being at a middle school teaching technology . . . you know, my first lessons in the garden. We did a dissection of seeds, like corn and lima beans, and I might have had something else. And we did a lab underneath this propagation area where they dissected and put the parts up. And they loved it. I mean, they stayed with me engaged for 45 minutes. Wow. And this was amazing. You don't keep kids . . . that engaged, and I'm a new . . . teacher at this school. So, I have no credibility. Yeah. I could be like everyone else—come in two weeks and leave. But they went with me. It was awesome. That's when I was, like, "yeah, that's it. This is it. This is where they want to learn."

Dissecting corn kernels sounds surprisingly engaging while still being relevant to learning basic plant anatomy.

Corn also plays a central role in one of the more controversial lessons taught in the edible schoolyards. One of the schools is an urban school located a few miles from the city center. Founded in 1916, the school does have a rich history, but it currently resides in a high-poverty area typical of urban landscapes. As described by one program specialist, some of the students' homes "can be like a hotel room, you know, where you got a hot plate, not a whole kitchen, and she [the teacher] is, like, 'I can show them how to make nutritious, at least reasonably nutritious, food out of cans.'"

In this lesson, the kitchen staff deliberately use canned goods such as corn and do not use fruits and vegetables grown in the gardens, recognizing that fresh produce is not necessarily available to students and families at home. Indeed, while this lesson is set in an urban school, many communities, even in this agriculturally rich region, do not have access to fresh seasonal produce either because it is simply not available in the stores, or it is available but unaffordable. Additionally, even when the produce is available, resources to prepare the produce, such as stoves and kitchens supplied with knives and cutting boards and counter space, are not available: hence this educator's intentional inclusion of canned corn and beans and other ingredients that are cheap and available to high-poverty communities, even available through food banks. The canned goods are mixed with herbs such as oregano that are readily available in neighborhood markets to prepare reasonably nutritious and far more delicious meals. Of course, herbs from the school's own garden can then be sent home with students to further the lesson. The lesson is obviously controversial among the edible schoolyard community but is explained and defended by Sofia:

> These children don't have access to a lot of fresh vegetables. And I said, "Listen, you can make a good vegetable soup out of cans. And I want to show these kids how to do it." The fresh vegetables were onion, celery, and garlic. Everything else came out of cans: beans, corn, tomatoes. It was one of the favorites here. And I'm, like, "Okay, well, when you're in your little hotel [with] a hot plate," because, at the time, I was cooking in a third grade classroom on a hot plate, "you can make this, you know."

The benefits in building student competence toward nutrition and flavor using resources available to them at home should not be overlooked.

Autonomy

In self-determination theory, autonomy refers to feeling that one's behaviors are self-endorsed, or congruent with one's authentic interests. In a school setting, autonomy can take many forms. On an individual student basis, autonomy can be promoted as students engaging in learning that they perceive as valuable and relevant to their own lives. In this manner, autonomy can be closely linked to competence. The student who has competently learned how to use a knife or utilize ingredients readily available to them, even if those ingredients are canned, has simultaneously taken a step toward living a fuller existence as an individual or autonomous person.

Issues of autonomy also arise from a curricular perspective, especially in our age of standardization. Like the principal who said, "It's fine to plant flowers, but let's plant basic skills first" (Ylimaki, 2012, p. 327), educators routinely have to face the pressure of bowing to the required content and timelines, relentlessly marching toward the inevitable exams, or seizing those, "aha!" moments as they arise. Because of their experiential nature, both the gardens and kitchens inherently provide more opportunities for things to go awry. Because of their outdoor location, the gardens provide more opportunity for distraction and even disruption. Yet those times when things go catawampus compared to the prepared lesson script can form some of the most relevant experiences in developing autonomy. In fact, Diego, who designs curriculum for the edible schoolyard network, recognizes this reality:

> If the opportunity comes up for a new experience or exploratory opportunity to happen, it really is a coordinated [effort] of the educators, whether you capitalize on that or not. And I think that's where we train our team to be

> able to see [that] in the garden, you're in the natural world. You're sitting there, trying a plant a lesson with a group of students. And then a hawk flies over, right? Yeah, the students [are] distracted. It's easier to divert and talk about, you know, . . . what the hawk's doing or what he has going on, and then getting back to the lesson. So, I think that those are times when students are able to break the curriculum, break the format, because we're there for them.

Diego notes that the curriculum he writes for the gardens and kitchens serves not as a step-by-step guide or a simple recipe for the educational experience, but rather as a "baseline" from which the teacher can and should deviate, as opportunities for authentic and engaging education arise. Diego continues by highlighting some of these impromptu experiences he has seen in both the kitchen and garden:

> Yeah, my memory sort of thinks in terms of those, you know, true experiences that I've seen [with] students. . . . I think I can speak generally on the topic because I've seen them happen so many times. There are a couple that stand out in particular, but I think that generally speaking, when it comes to our program, and this goes for the garden and the kitchen, our . . . job as educators and as leaders, leading these students in this experience is to really not [be] bound by a curriculum, not to be bound by a lesson, but [to] build the lesson as a baseline. . . . And I want them to experience that. So, it's as simple . . . as just the ant or a bug on a leaf and everybody wants to go over and look at it: "Okay, we're going to stop doing what we're doing over here and focus on this because we can take that path of discovery of the students."

Flexibility to build upon autonomous experiences then can be incorporated into the lessons by design, such as deliberately allowing space for students to experiment with different spices and even providing the opportunity for diverse spices that represent the diverse cultures of the classroom, leading to discovery and discussion of different cultures. Or, the autonomy arises when a hawk flies overhead as described by Sandy:

> There's always things that come up that you didn't plan for, whether, it's a really annoying leaf blower across the street [author's note, this is literally happening as I type this] or it's, like, all of a sudden a hawk flies over the gar-

> den, or they found a praying mantis, or something that you just didn't plan for but it's capturing the students' attention . . . Rather than ignoring that, make it a teachable moment and have them observe it, ask questions, and share what they are thinking.

Hawks flying overhead must be rather common, as they were mentioned by several garden educators, including one who shared a story in which the students and teacher all witnessed a hawk attack another bird. These things happen in nature. Insects also happen in nature and form another favorite impromptu lesson: When bees appeared in garden session, some students wanted to immediately kill them. The garden educators utilized the sudden appearance to explain how to react safely around bees and their importance to the life cycle. White cabbage moths, however, are not welcome in the garden, as they lay their eggs on the garden plants, and the eggs hatch into hungry caterpillars. The eggs and caterpillars must be picked off the plants. But all is not lost, as the chickens are quite fond of the caterpillars, and their inclusion in the fowl's diet results in more nutritious chicken eggs.

The key in developing autonomy through this flexibility is perhaps found in the educator using the new development to guide the students. In other words, the educator does not have to sagely know all the answers about hawks or praying mantises or hornworms (to name a few distractions mentioned by edible schoolyard educators), but rather needs to be prepared to ask, "what did you observe?" and, "what questions do you have?" and, "what are you thinking about this?"

These same questions can work as well in the kitchen as they can in the garden. Paisley, a kitchen educator, describes some of the kitchen mishaps and her reaction to them:

> There have definitely been times where, like, okay, "you guys dropped the vinaigrette. And it's too late to make another one, and you guys are running around, so no vinaigrette for us. I'm sorry." I kind of sat back, and I was, like, "you just have to figure it out." It was a fourth-grade class, and towards this time of the year, I do like to put the responsibility on them. Okay. I was, like, "how long have you been coming here? Kindergarten, okay. What do you do in the kitchen?" "Okay," I was, like, "you don't need me anymore. Like, I want to see you guys. If you need to know what to do, what do you do? What do you look for in the recipe?" If [they] need to set up the table,

> because we have table managers too, they can set up; they can do all of it by themselves. So, there have been times . . . the last time that happened was the minute grab: They dropped it, so they had to improvise, and they just added the olive oil on the salt and the pepper, and they tossed it together. And yeah, we put it in our salad; it was garden salad tacos. So that was the last time, I mean they . . . did it. They were upset because there had been a great drop on the floor, and it was a whole cup of oil, but it was an oil slick. . . . I was really mad because I was meant to get a "sorry" for that. Um, but [they'll] never do it again. I can assure you that.

Paisley goes on to describe that there were tears and crying over the spilled vinaigrette. However, she used the opportunity to explain and coach the kids in the organized chaos that is a kitchen and that there is no use in crying over spilled milk (or vinaigrette as the case might be). The same coaching and questions can apply when students add too much salt, too little salt, and other kitchen mishaps.

Relatedness

Vinaigrette, simple salad dressing made from an emulsion of oil such as olive, an acid such as balsamic vinegar, and herbs such as those grown in the garden, symbolically represents relatedness, as the various ingredients are each valuable on their own yet combine to create a community of texture and flavors that exceed the sum of the parts. So do salads. Salads form a favorite kitchen activity for educators and students alike based on a number of factors. Salads can be easily created from the fresh produce grown in the garden. The acidic ingredient in the vinaigrette can be a citrus, such as lemons grown in the garden, as shared by principal Luca: "They made a citrus vinaigrette on their salad and tied that to literally talking about vitamin C and the importance of it." Salads can be easily produced in the kitchen, even with young students. Salads do not require any raw meats that need cooking, which in turn greatly simplifies the kitchen's ability to meet health codes. Many community health codes are far more stringent when a public facility, such as a school kitchen, handles raw meats than if the kitchen limits itself to fruits, vegetables, and perhaps pre-cooked meats. However, pre-cooked meats are usually not very healthy, think hot dogs, and so do not really meet the mission of the edible schoolyards. Meat is also not utilized to help save costs on ingredients. Lydia provides additional insights into the value of salads:

> In the kitchen, . . . one of the lessons that I did appreciate the most was when they would make salads at times. The salad was not the priority, but we did have salads. They were excellent, amazingly excellent [at] choosing the ingredients to create a vinaigrette without a recipe, like measuring appropriate ratios and the whole works because they've done it so many times. So, they were able to create their own flavor profiles and create their own salad dressings, which was so cool to see because so many kids don't [have] experiences in the kitchen because their parents don't feel confident that their child can do it. Right. It gave them that confidence, and they just ran with it. So, they had a strong sense of ownership and leadership in our garden and in our kitchen.

Another take on the use of a variety of vegetables cooked to combine a new whole, greater than the individual parts due to the ingredients' relatedness, revolves around stir-fries, as shared by Jasper, a special education classroom teacher:

> So normally, it depends on whatever's in season, so they also teach them if they're gonna make a salad or they're gonna make some type of Chinese food, some type of vegetables or anything, . . . it just depends really [on] what's in season and what they have accessible to be able to provide to the families. So, I know that the recipes prior to COVID were switched off depending on what was growing in the garden.

Sofia also discusses Asian food, particularly an Asian noodle salad, as one of her favorite kitchen lessons as it draws from the bok choy they grow in the garden.

The inclusion of a variety of cultures' foods into the kitchen experience creates another opportunity for relatedness. The schools with edible schoolyards in this study represent diverse student communities, including Mexican immigrants, as we have already seen through the leadership, but also include a variety of other cultures, both immigrant and long-established. The schools represent the region's thriving Indian community, many recently immigrated from the India's Punjab region, and Asian communities including Chinese and Korean influences. As Diego explains:

> So oftentimes, you know, let's say we're making . . . a recipe, right? And a student talks about their, let's say it's a . . . [student] of Indian descent, right?

> And they talk about all of the spices and the dishes of their mom and grandma, or their family might cook at home, and we can incorporate some of that into the end of the recipe almost immediately because we have this on hand. [It's] not necessarily to accommodate; it's more so to experience. Okay, this student has an experience that they want to bring into the space the student hasn't experienced, so when it comes to the kitchen, there's always that opportunity to start tweaking and playing with different dressings and different flavors, and we get to see the entire world influence lessons, and that's where we can kind of go off the beaten path and have these new experiences with students.

The food in the kitchens, and the ingredients grown in the gardens, intentionally reflect these diverse influences, such as the inclusion of the Asian noodle salad, spicy Thai, chow mein, and garden salad tacos.

James, an activity leader, shared how the kitchen experiences take the food to another cultural level by intentionally teaching the students how to use chopsticks when they prepare the Asian noodle salad. Here, the food represents cultural diversity, but how it is served and consumed furthers the cultural experience. In addition to cooking in the kitchen, the students also follow a set protocol for setting the table, sitting together, and talking while consuming their meals. Things are kept positive, as already indicated, by the prohibition of saying foods are yucky or otherwise not liked, although students are allowed to say it is "not my favorite" after at least trying it. Students are assigned to various roles related to mealtimes, including setting the table and clearing the table. The roles rotate to ensure an equitable distribution and opportunity. Tables are often covered with tablecloths. During the meal, students draw from a premade deck of index cards, each card containing a conversation starter. The net effect, in the words of one educator, is to recreate the friendly, welcoming, collegial atmosphere of a favorite local restaurant.

The edible schoolyard's potential for building a welcoming atmosphere extends beyond the student experience to students' parents and even the local community. Sloane, a kitchen educator, shares:

> [The wood-fired pizza is everyone's] favorite. All teachers include it, and again, I think just because you're including it would fire up and . . . you're including a food . . . that everyone loves, and the kids also experience it in a different way because it's not your typical pepperoni pizza. You know, we

> don't cook with meat in the schoolyard. But, they get to make it like a garden pizza and use all the vegetables that are in season to make their toppings, and they are in it 100%. They help us make the dough, the sauce, and then, you know, chop the toppings, and then you have, like, assembly day where they assemble, and we enjoy again as a family outside with the wood fire and just, you know, enjoying each other's company.

The wood-fired pizzas are not just for students and educators but also feature prominently in parent nights, such as an end-of-the-year pizza party. As the pandemic started, principal Hayden started another community trend by initiating his own community cooking show via Zoom:

> So, [when the] pandemic occurred, what we thought was, why not look at it as an opportunity? It was six months into our administrative leadership. Our team had taken the reins from the prior [principal], who is a good friend of mine, and we [wondered], "How could we make it virtual so that the students and the families can still have that experience?" So, we were thinking SEL [socio-emotional learning], and someone said, "Why don't we create a virtual cooking and gardening class?"

Hayden ran out to the local grocery store and purchased some ingredients to supplement what they had from the garden and returned to the school. Incidentally, this is occurring in the same rural community with only one grocery store, and that store was influenced to start carrying fresher, more seasonal, and a wider selection of produce as demand for fresh fruits and vegetables increased due to the edible schoolyard's influence. Returning to Hayden's moment of inspiration, he returned to the school, gathered the edible schoolyard teachers, set up a Zoom feed and:

> What was on the menu for the day was processed ham, goat cheese, and you know, artichoke, and it was just little items, and I did everything on tinfoil and plastic. . . . I might have set off the smoke alarm, and it was hilarious. But from there, it just went like wildfire. Next thing I know, the very next day, they had set up, you know, an elaborate studio. But what came out of it is, we were then able to purchase, I don't know if you know this, but we would purchase all the supplies needed. We'd send out an invite for anyone in the community. Here's the . . . recipe that we're cooking, that our ESY

> team will be preparing; here are all the ingredients. Why don't you enjoy this? Come pick up your ingredients at X time; the Zoom will occur that night or . . . whenever that scheduled meeting is. And so, families, . . . we would have students come and families come, and you would see a Zoom, if you could turn on your camera, of all these kids cooking and their parents cooking together.

This Zoom experience grew across the edible schoolyard network with other schools creating their own Zoom classes. Sometimes, the Zoom would be like a cooking show with the edible schoolyard staff demonstrating the recipes while parents and children followed along at home. At other times, parents and children would be invited to the kitchen and prepare the meals together while the event was also streamed for those who preferred to join from home.

These school productions eventually grew into a local news channel doing a weekly morning segment on their show where they did a cooking demonstration using the edible schoolyard ingredients. The Zoom shows also led the schools to identify further pathways toward local community impact. In order to cook at home, what is being shown via the Zoom feed, ingredients are needed. This led the schools to begin creating grocery bags of the ingredients that needed to be drawn from the garden. During the pandemic, parents could stop by the school and pick up a bag at a set time. Following the pandemic, the practice has continued but also includes distributing bags of produce to parents regardless of whether or not there is a Zoom show. The gardens produce a plethora of fruits and vegetables, and the excess that is not needed for the school kitchen is distributed to parents who want fresh produce as they wait in their cars in the after-school pickup line or to those who wish to stop by the school for a bag. That the produce contained in the bags is the same produce the kids are using in the kitchens provides a further opportunity for parents and their children to cook together at home. The child can even serve as lead chef using the skills learned in the kitchen.

Relatedness, or socialization, using more Deweyesque terminology, grows from the edible schoolyards in a variety of student-, school-, family-, and community-centered ways, as does autonomy and competence. While these concepts have been presented here as three distinct processes, any given lesson can promote all three simultaneously, even if one concept might be more strongly represented at any given moment.

References

Dewey, J., & Dewey, E. (1962). *Schools of tomorrow*. E.P. Dutton & Co., Inc. (Original work published 1915).

Knoll, M. (2022). *Beyond rhetoric: New perspectives on John Dewey's pedagogy*. International Academic Publishers.

Ylimaki, R. M. (2012). Curriculum leadership in a conservative era. *Educational Administration Quarterly, 48*(2), 304–346. https://doi.org/10.1177/0013161X11427393

CHAPTER SEVEN

BREAKING DOWN THE WALLS BETWEEN EDIBLE SCHOOLYARDS AND CLASSROOMS

SCHOOL GARDENS AND KITCHENS have at least a century-old tradition of providing real-world, child-centered, and engaging educational experiences as seen from Dewey's time to Alice Waters' work, to the edible schoolyards of today. Educators representing a variety of roles in the gardens, kitchens, classrooms, and front office from across the four schools in this study report a diversity of favorite activities. Student survey results show a positive view of the gardens and kitchens that grows with their participation in edible schoolyard activities. The edible schoolyard experiences of students and educators alike correspond to the goals of developing competence, autonomy, and relatedness, the three key components of cultivating self-determination.

Yet, in today's educational environment, this is not enough. School leaders today are accountable to the standards assessed through standardized testing. Educators faced with meeting the accountability requirements of standardized testing are faced with two broad choices. On the one hand, as new professional managers, they may lead their schools in utilizing prepared, packaged, skill-and-drill, or chalk-and-talk test prep curricular materials, an approach exemplified by the principal who finds it fine to plant flowers, as long as basic skills are planted first (Ylimaki, 2012). For this principal, basic skills and gardening oppose each other, with gardening implicitly suggested as an inferior educational path. Therefore, the new professional manager chooses rote learning type exercises that can be tightly aligned with the standardized tests themselves, often these exercises have research backing up their effectiveness in raising test scores if implemented with fidelity, and can be purchased for immediate implementation. On the other hand, as curriculum developers, school leaders may wish to invest their limited resources into working with the community to develop authentic, real-world, and engaging projects that also promise to produce improved results on the standardized tests. School gardens and kitchens provide a specific pathway toward engaging and authentic project-based learning. This is the realm of the edible schoolyard.

So far, the question of critical curriculum leadership versus new professional management has been presented as a binary choice of one or the other. In the real world, especially with the inescapable testing requirements and their public displays of accountability through state dashboards and various media, and the opportunity for parents to move their children to other schools that perform better on these accepted tests, there is an ever-present market challenge. Thus, the contrast of critical curriculum leadership and new professional management might be better viewed as a continuum. To what extent can the edible schoolyards representing engaging education collaborate with the regular classrooms representing the core academics by which school success is measured? To what extent do the edible schoolyards help or hinder the work of the classrooms? This chapter explores the relationship between the edible schoolyards and the classrooms by focusing on garden and kitchen experiences that inform, support, and enhance the knowledge and skills required by the Common Core standards. Insights into the overall school impact, as seen in publicly available standardized testing results, are explored, and suggestions for the intentional collaboration needed to break down the walls between edible schoolyards and classrooms are provided.

The edible schoolyards in this study are supported in part by the Grimm Family Educational Foundation whose mission includes building vibrant communities, improving the health of students and families, creating economic growth in the community, and closing the achievement gap (Grimm Family, 2018). The expectations of the edible schoolyards are founded in growing flowers but also building basic skills. One effect of this vision is seen through the words of Diego, a program director from the Edible Schoolyard Kern County, who shares:

> We have recently done some interviews, job interviews for a summer internship position, and one of the interns came to us with some, you know,

> experience, and a cover letter said that she had been a student at one of his [elementaries] and then showed up and started talking to us about her life and what she's doing now. And, she . . . has been at the edible schoolyard from fourth to sixth grade. So, now she's an adult . . . and in college. She's in her first year of college, and she's ready to start developing a career path. And sure enough, she's a plant science major [and] after Bakersfield College, hoping to go into plant genetics someday.

The connections between the garden and the academics of the classroom are obvious. This is not about growing flowers at the expense of learning fractions; this is about learning through doing to be better situated for ongoing educational achievement and so much more. Diego continues:

> Then we kept talking. She started her own [home garden], and she has this huge inspiration for it, and . . . there's the direct link, right between the work and what she was exposed to as a child . . . getting to experience that as a student, and then . . . for that to inspire her. . . . She then brought that back home and started her own home garden; . . . she's our prime example of what we want to see. And then she has a huge influence in cooking. In every interview, I start with, I ask, if you were to have us over for dinner this evening, what would you . . . be preparing for us? And she talked about how she used fresh seasonal produce. And it was like, oh my gosh, we were able to influence a student that's now an adult to make these choices.

The vision of a college-going culture and creating better life opportunities, fulfilling the promise of America, but also doing so in a manner that promotes health and well-being within a community seeks to fulfill the promise of Dewey's vision for education.

Carson is the Chief Executive Officer of the charter school network, which includes two of the four study schools. Carson seeks to operationalize the mission:

> So yeah, so as CEO, I work with, . . . through our office as management of their schools, working principals. And through that, we work on program; we work on ensuring that there's some type of integration. We haven't quite found the sweet spot, but how do we inform Common Core Next Gen standards and how does what's happening in the garden [address them]. . . . We haven't cracked the code yet. It's a lot of effort and working together.

> So, there's . . . safety and quality control from the standpoint of scheduling, working with the foundation on putting together a curriculum with some metrics the last couple of years, and . . . outcomes and measures to measure the outcomes and how do we know what's working right, . . . how we know what's effective.

Carson, as the CEO, is setting a vision and tone for the day-to-day work of the kitchen, garden, and classroom educators within the charter school organization. That tone is one of finding the "sweet spot" of integrating the Common Core and Next Generation Science Standards into what is happening within the experiences of the gardens and kitchens. Whether by default or design, Carson is operating as a critical curriculum developer, looking for the natural connections between engaging and authentic experiences in the gardens and kitchens and how these experiential learning experiences can inform and support the metrics of standardized accountability. He is not interested in having students grow flowers or carrots for simply the growth's sake, but rather is interested in knowing, "How do we know what is effective?" in what they are doing. Carson also touches on the ongoing and iterative nature of this critical curriculum work by admitting, "we haven't cracked the code yet." The nature of child-centered education serving a diversity of students suggests there actually is not a code to be cracked, at least not while staying true to diverse community needs. Instead, the critical curriculum educator looks first to what is authentic and engaging to the students, but also addresses real needs of competency in learning reading, math, science, history, and other subjects, and then makes natural connections back to the standards. Carson further explores this tension between child-centered work in the edible schoolyards and accountability to standards:

> The realities of standardized accountability to the organization's viability comes through clearly. To maintain our authorization, we have to meet certain metrics each year on state testing. And that's a reality in charter schools. It should be, right? There's accountability. And here's an alternative, and it should be a better alternative by some quantifiable metric. So that's a reality.

Still, they are trying "to have the best of both worlds now," and he even admits that when he arrived about seven years ago, the system, despite the garden and kitchen's presence, was more heavily "kill and drill," related to the test prep. In other words, even with the fantastic facilities available, the program still leaned into traditional rote learning. To address this, Carson is looking for more "authentic assessments," revolving around academic concepts.

The gardens provide a plethora of opportunities for learning various sciences, especially biology, and the theme of life cycles surfaces repeatedly among garden educators. Carson, shifted in the interview from CEO to parent, as his child attends one of the edible schoolyard schools, and discussed how his child became fascinated with seeds through lessons at school. They now have created a garden at home based on this interest. His daughter plans on studying plant science in college, so gardening is more than just a hobby but rather a gateway to future education. Jose provides more detail into lifecycles through the lens of hornworms and moths. Jose, the garden educator who left a career designing satellites for an aerospace company to work in an edible schoolyard in a rural school, further illustrates the intentionality of connecting standards and real-world experiences. One of the Common Core state standards relates to life cycles. Here, the students one day found a tomato hornworm, a rather large and nasty looking pest that can devour and destroy plants within days. Jose captured the hornworm and brought it to the classroom teacher who obtained one of the little cages in which butterflies can grow. The hornworm was introduced to its new home within the classroom and within weeks had progressed through its life cycle to the chrysalis stage before emerging as a moth. Completing the life cycle the students and their teacher had been observing, the moth was released back into the garden. Jose noted with fondness and bit of awe at the students' learning about life cycles by recounting that every time they returned to the garden, the students asked, "How is our butterfly doing?" and "Is it still alive?" and "Can we go look for it?" (The students, kindergartners, will need a bit more coaching to learn the difference between a butterfly and a moth!)

Within this life cycle demonstration, however, lies another key academic concept critical to the college-going culture Jose is intentionally promoting with his elementary school charges. Comparison and contrast thinking, along with evaluating based on data, form key thinking abilities for academic growth. The hornworm is clearly a pest, as it destroys needed crops. Yet, not all insects are pests; some are beneficial. The comparison and contrast thinking, along with evaluative thinking inherent in the exercise, are developed through the insect lessons with kids as young as kindergarten.

Likewise, recognizing patterns is cultivated through the garden experience. Again, with the kindergartners, Jose and the garden staff give the students different bulbs, such as tulips and daffodils, which in and of themselves represent different shapes. These different flowering bulbs are then planted in different patterns which the students can easily observe when the plants grow and bloom later in the spring. The experience of handling, planting, and nurturing the plants creates an experiential connection between students and plants, allows them to see the life cycle in action, and can leverage into more meta-cognitive thinking regarding the patterns created by the flowers' various shapes, sizes, and planting arrangements.

Higher grades also experience similar applications. One year, Jose recollects, the fifth graders were working on creating histograms. It was December, maybe even early January, and oranges were in season. The students harvested the oranges which came off the tree in varying sizes unlike the uniform, sorted consistency found in supermarkets. Following the harvest, students sorted the oranges by weight and created their histograms which they then presented to their classmates. Jose did not mention that everyone would later enjoy freshly squeezed orange juice after this exercise in pattern making, categorizing, measuring, evaluating, graphing, and public presentation, but he did continue the breakfast theme by illustrating another example using eggs.

Here, the classroom teacher collaborated with garden staff and the garden's 12 chickens. The chickens are different sizes and different breeds and lay different-sized eggs. In the classroom, the students began by researching online and through teacher-provided materials how eggs are graded for commercial sale. This is the system which results in the large AA or similar type labels found on all eggs readily available in a supermarket. This portion of the assignment involves reading but also research, as the students explore United States Department of Agriculture standards for egg classification. Equipped with their new knowledge about egg grading, the students headed to the chicken coop where they collected eggs and proceeded to use their measurement and assessment tools to grade the eggs. Final reports were written and presented to the class, thus ensuring the essential communication skills of writing and public speaking were also practiced.

Another garden educator, Valerie, builds upon the theme of systems thinking by emphasizing ecosystems. In one disruptive moment during a garden class, a bee flew out and caused some consternation among the students.

Yet, this moment turned teachable through a discussion regarding the role bees play in the ecosystem and the connections among bees, pollination, growth, and reproduction. Kids are taught to understand and respect bees. As they learn the connections, the "lightbulbs go off," in Valerie's words, regarding how bees are related to the food they are growing and eventually will eat. When animals in one part of the ecosystem are wiped out, there is an effect on the rest of the system.

Note here that there are developing connections between the content in the garden and academic STEM concepts, in this case the ecosystem. But the connections are even bigger as the kids are learning through the ecosystem the concept of systems thinking, the connections among things and concepts, and that effects in one part of a system, whether that system is the garden, the environment, or a computer, affect other parts. Dewey, through his picture of the relatedness of the garden to the classroom to the community, effectively was showing a networked or connected educational system with the interrelated parts affecting and being affected by one another. A stray bee can lead to a discussion about pollination, which then leads to learning about the anatomy of the flower, which then leads to seeds and the plant as a whole, which then leads to both how the plant contributes food and also oxygen to support our own lives. Upon harvest and consumption, the plant then turns into compost, which involves both good and bad bacteria as it transforms into fertilizer to begin the next cycle.

In the process of this scientific study, connections are made to history and geography in addition to the aforementioned science-related concepts. The plant is part of a broader food chain for other creatures in its environment and for humans, including the students. Because of the plant's importance as a food source, the importance of stewardship is emphasized. This concept of stewardship, in turn, leads to discussion about cover cropping and the importance of maintaining the soil.

Historically, not paying attention to the soil combined with drought conditions and heavy winds led to the Dust Bowl that affected the Great Plains area and contributed to the Great Depression of the 1930s. This ecological and agricultural disaster affected millions directly through the literal loss of the soil upon which their farms depended. This disaster contributed to the local economy, history, and agriculture of the Central Valley, where our study schools are located, as the displaced "Oakies" sought new opportunity through their westward migration. (Kiger, 2023). Hence, the garden experience regarding caring for the plants and the soil in which they grow can turn into a local, state, and national history lesson involving the Great Depression, economics, westward migration, and a lesson in how the local community developed.

The gardens and the kitchens provide experiences that lead to student questions as they engage with their environment. In one example, students in the garden noticed it was getting dark earlier as the year wore on and asked why. (It's hard to imagine students noticing a difference in sunlight in already darkened classrooms with a focus on screen-based learning.) The teachers from both the garden and the regular classroom seized on this interest to lead exploration of the movement of the sun, seasons, and Ben Franklin creating time zones for commerce reasons.

Students also ask questions in the kitchen. "What would happen if we substituted raspberries for blackberries in this recipe?" "The blackberries have too many seeds; we need raspberries here." (Note the evaluative thinking and systems thinking here, as the seeds affect the system of the recipe.) "Why are these beans long while the snap peas are not? What is the difference?" "Why can't we have a banana tree?" "Well, kids, let's go research why not; or maybe why we could." As it turns out, banana trees can actually be grown in this region, but they may need so much attention it's not worth the effort. But here, the teacher and the student alike become learners in a student-driven, real-world, authentic mini research project that involves botany, geography, agriculture, and economics.

Following recipes provides a plethora of opportunities for engaging academic standards in real-world contexts. One recipe called for the dish to come out sweet, but the students in one group wanted to try something more savory. So, they modified the recipe on the fly and produced a more savory result, which they "loved," according to Stella and Julian, two classroom teachers. The teachers then capitalized on this mini experiment by leading further classroom discussion on flavor profiles and why some things work, and some don't. Measurements form the core of many recipes, and many measurements require a working knowledge of fractions. Mixing up a tablespoon and a teaspoon measurement will have a big impact on the recipe's outcome. So would using the wrong fraction, such as mixing up a quarter-tablespoon and a half-tablespoon of an ingredient such as salt. Paisley, a kitchen educator from a rural school, recounts how the kitchen educators compare measurements to money, such as a quarter is one-fourth of a dollar, and can illustrate with the measuring cups placed at each station. Still, sometimes students make mistakes such as adding too much salt to the cornbread, which in at least one case led to the bread being "inedible." In Paisley's recollection, the students tried the bread and "were, like, what?" Yet, a learning moment occurred as Paisley walked the students through the measurement process again, and they realized their mistake. All found the situation "funny."

Jasper, a special education teacher from a rural school, provided another important insight regarding recipes. The Common Core standards that form the basis of the state standardized tests require students to learn reading, and in doing so, emphasize reading informational texts over other forms of reading such as poetry and short stories. Informational texts are a form of nonfiction writing designed to inform the reader about a specific topic. Most textbooks are informational texts, as are many how-to manuals. This emphasis on informational texts leads to the question of, functionally speaking, what sort of informational text does one put on a standardized test for early primary grades? As it turns out, recipes form great informational text for standardized tests. They are short enough to include in a test where time is important; yet they adequately examine students' ability to comprehend the information presented. Recipes are essentially mini how-to manuals and can range in complexity from basic, appropriate to primary grades, to much more complex. The kitchen educators did not use recipes with their students because recipes would appear on the standardized tests. They used recipes for the authentic and real-world experience recipes provided. That recipes also happen to be on the standardized test and that students had actual experience reading and using recipes serves as an example of how authentic experiences can be connected to future testing without losing the experiences and authenticity.

Jasper's story regarding recipes being used in both the kitchens and the tests raises the question of how effective this kitchen-based education might actually be as measured on the standardized tests. The rural charter school Jasper works at is rather new, and as such, there is not a lot of testing data. The state suspension of standardized testing during the COVID-19 pandemic further limits the available data. That schools across the state suffered precipitous drops in testing scores upon resumption of testing following the pandemic calls into question the validity of post-pandemic testing (Chapman, 2022). Therefore, testing from the spring of 2019 provides the most accurate snapshot of available data and is presented in Table 7.1.

	School	School Growth	State	State Growth
All Students	11.4 below	29.9 plus	2.5 below	3.7 plus
English Learners	41.6 below	34.6 plus	45.1 below	3.1 plus
Hispanic	10.6 below	30.9 plus	26.6 below	4.5 plus
Socioeconomically Disadvantaged	16.9 below	30.8 plus	30.1 below	4.4 plus
Student With Disabilities	65.9 below	46.4 plus	88.1 below	7.9 plus

Note: Data from the California School Dashboard (2023) https://www.caschooldashboard.org/

TABLE 7.1. English Language Arts Standardized Testing Scores by Demographic Group, 2019

This table tells a mixed yet encouraging story regarding the relationship between real-world learning and standardized testing. On the story's downside, the overall English Language Arts (ELA) scores for the school overall and for each major student sub-group in 2019 fell below the state standard, ranging from 10.6 points below for Hispanic students to 65.9 points below for Student With Disabilities. Yet, the state averages were also below expectations, ranging from 2.5 points below standard for all students to 88.1 points below for Students With Disabilities. Here then, the story of our recipe-using edible schoolyard school starts to look better as Students With Disabilities scored 22.2 points higher than the state average. Further, the growth scores also tell an encouraging story. All Students and students in every sub-category in both the edible schoolyard school and the state average showed growth from 2018 to the results presented in 2019. The edible schoolyard students at this school showed substantially more growth than their peers statewide. For example, Students With Disabilities at the edible schoolyard school showed 46.4 points of growth, which is 38.5 points more growth than their peers statewide (California School Dashboard, 2023). While much further research is needed, the results from 2019 nevertheless suggest that real-world activities such as using recipes in a kitchen may relate to student academic growth.

The urban school in this study provides another perspective on the relationship between edible schoolyard education and standardized test results. James, a garden educator, mentions that his school's math scores went "through the roof" when the edible schoolyard started. Unlike the new charter school represented in the last example, this school had been built in 1916, right around the time Dewey was writing, but did not implement their edible schoolyard until the 2018-2019 schoolyear. Table 7.2 presents the three years of standardized testing data for the school as a whole in the three years leading up to COVID-19 and including the year the edible schoolyard was implemented (California School Dashboard, 2023).

	ELA	Mathematics
2016-2017	77.3 Below	86.2 Below
2017-2018	70.2 Below	74.5 Below
2018-2019	49.4 Below	65.8 Below

Note: Data from the California School Dashboard (2023) https://www.caschooldashboard.org/

TABLE 7.2. Testing in ELA and Mathematics, 2016-2019

Again, the results are mixed but hold promise for the mission of closing the achievement gap as measured by standardized test scores. This urban school has consistently performed below the state average, yet in 2018-2019 when the edible schoolyard was fully operational for the first time, ELA scores jumped 20.8 points and mathematics showed a smaller but still impressive 8.7-point increase. Mathematics had also seen an increase during the previous years, which suggests more than just the edible schoolyard experiences were ongoing in the school. Still, the edible schoolyard experiences did not hurt this growth trend in math, and the 20-point increase in English Language Arts during the first year of implementation cannot be ignored (California School Dashboard, 2023).

That the test scores improved for the first year of the edible schoolyard's implementation at this urban school is perhaps even more impressive because the school was looking at the edible schoolyard more as a resource to support socio-emotional learning than as an academic resource. In the words of the school's principal, Kylie, who oversaw the edible schoolyard's implementation:

> It has really been a learning year for me in terms of what the edible schoolyard can bring to our students . . . coming from a school similar as a vice principal, similar demographics, similar social economic status of our stu-

> dents. . . . I can see the difference. The experience our students have is so well rounded, and it really does play into their day. So, if that draws me, I'm really interested in looking more into the social-emotional aspect and that connection to the edible schoolyard and farm-to-table program. I feel that we naturally do that here because we have a big focus on social-emotional learning . . . that applies to the garden and kitchen program [and] is of interest to me moving forward. And then just looking at, you know, our just disciplinary indicators . . . you know, it's interesting to look at where we are at this point in the year [compared to] other schools who don't have these types of programs. We have much lower levels of discipline. And the reason I can compare that is because I was at a school very similar where we had much higher levels of disciplinary issues. So, I was pleasantly surprised when I came to [this school], because there is . . . it tends to have this reputation: "Oh, you're going to make headway? Oh, good luck." I'm really working to change that reputation because that's not what it's like at all.

While there was an emphasis on socio-emotional learning in the initial vision at this particular school, there were also intentional academic connections. Kylie talked about connections with vocabulary between the edible schoolyard and the classrooms. Students also created a number of graphs based on their kitchen experiences, such as conducting a tasting, recording student answers, and building graphs from their own data. Kylie also supported another school initiative, Project Lead the Way, in working with the garden to start a farmers market from garden produce where students designed labels and handled money. In terms of other initiatives, Lydia, an edible schoolyard project manager, talked about her efforts to connect classrooms and schoolyards:

> Maybe I'm a micromanager, but signage in a garden and our kitchen is hugely important. The kids need to know what the crop is in the ground and the bed. I wanted our signage to be even more extensive in terms of listing how long [a plant] takes to grow, indicators that [help us] know that it's ready to harvest, conditions that plant needs to thrive, so that in the garden, there's a real world piece of literature or piece of information . . . informational text . . . that [students] need to read, to be able to understand and help support that plant. And so, for me, signage is important in the kitchen when you're saying, "hey, go grab a colander." Well, there probably should be some sort

> of labels [so] that . . . kids know what colanders are. So, signage is [a] huge . . . detail, but I think it really brings the literacy connection to what's happening with the lessons.

The implications for literacy are clear, especially for lower grades and also for those who are learning English. The gardens and kitchens with actual objects, some of which the students already recognize, and accompanying words create an authentic and natural environment for language acquisition whether students are learning to read for the first time or learning a new language, as is the case for English language learners.

Kylie's story about the comparison of the school to other neighborhood schools regarding reputation and discipline, in turn, suggests another angle of comparison regarding standardized testing. All schools in the edible schoolyard network are below the state average in their standardized testing results, although they are showing growth in closing the achievement gap. The problem, however, may not be in the performance of the schools but rather in inequities embedded in the standardized tests themselves. There has long been a negative relationship between high-poverty schools, such as those represented in this study, and academic achievement (e.g., Dietrichson et al., 2017; Harwell & LeBeau, 2010; Ilie et al., 2017; Sirin, 2005; White, 1982). Hence, comparing the edible schoolyard schools' achievement to the state averages might not form the most accurate evaluation of the edible schoolyard's relationship to standardized testing. Instead, comparing results from the edible schoolyard schools with their peer schools in the same community would provide another measure. This is done in Table 7.3 with the study schools indicated by an asterix (*).

The general trend in Table 7.3 indicates that the schools with edible schoolyards are performing higher than their peer schools in both growth and in how closely they approach or how far they exceed the state standards (California School Dashboard, 2023). More research is needed to assess exactly how the edible schoolyards impact standardized testing results, but for an educational leader seeking to implement an edible schoolyard at their school, standardized testing cannot be used as an excuse to not pursue the authentic, engaging, and child-centered experiences the gardens and kitchens provide.

	Demographic	ELA Performance	ELA Change	Math Performance	Math Change
ESY 1*	Rural	5.1 points below standard	22.3 points increase	26.9 points below standard	9.6 points increase
Peer 1	Rural	14.5 points below standard	9.2 points increase	29.4 points below standard	11.3 points increase
Peer 2	Rural	38.6 points below standard	13.6 points increase	66.3 points below standard	9.8 points increase
ESY 2*	Rural	11.4 points below standard	29.9 points increase	37.1 points below standard	11.7 points increase
Peer 1	Rural	55.6 points below standard	4.6 points decline	65.2 points below standard	0.9 points maintained
Peer 2	Rural	52.5 points below standard	6.9 points increase	70.8 points below standard	7.4 points decline
ESY 3*	Urban	49.4 points below standard	20.8 points increase	65.8 points below standard	8.6 points increase
Peer 1	Urban	49.1 points below standard	10.9 points increase	64.4 points below standard	18.3 points increase
Peer 2	Urban	23.9 points below standard	1.4 point maintained	53.5 points below standard	4.2 points increase
ESY 4*	Suburban	13.1 points above standard	1.4 points maintained	7.7 points below standard	11.8 points increase
Peer 1	Suburban	1.3 points below standard	12.3 points increase	16.2 points below standard	25.7 points increase
Peer 2	Suburban	5.7 points below standard	15.8 points decline	22.1 points below standard	1.7 points maintained

Note: Data from the California School Dashboard (2023) https://www.caschooldashboard.org/

TABLE 7.3. Results on California Assessment of Student Performance and Progress, Spring 2019

Using standardized testing as a reason to not include child-centered activity in the school experience may also have other unintended consequences. As already explored, standardized testing tends to focus on specific skills and concepts to the exclusion of other equally valuable learning. For example, the emphasis on informational text learning is valuable and needed, but so is learning that emphasizes literature, along with culture and history. Stella and Julian, two classroom teachers at one of the rural schools in the study, talk about how they have literature about Egypt and work with the kitchen educators to make the story come alive by preparing their own dukkah spice. Dukkah spice is featured in the story the students read in class and is an Egyptian spice formed by a blend of nuts, sesame seeds, coriander, and cumin which the students can prepare and eat in the kitchen. Some of the herbs in dukkah can be grown in the school garden. Almonds feature in some dukkah recipes and are a significant local agricultural crop, thus providing another local connection.

Stella and Julian also make connections between citrus, scurvy, and the book (Stevenson, 1883/2016):

> We read an abridged version of *Treasure Island* with our scholars, and we were able to connect with the kitchen. We extended the lesson and kind of taught them what scurvy was and how scurvy affected sailors or pirates, and so on, and we were able to bring a citrus-inspired recipe into it, and the kids ate up the lesson and the food. They loved it. I mean, to this day, they still mention scurvy. Like, if we talk about anything that, like . . . well, they're gonna get scurvy if they don't have their citrus. So, I mean, it's wonderful. Yeah, it's wonderful, the connections we're able to make between the classroom and, you know, . . . you can do it with ideas. You can do it with standards. You can do it with concepts. It's really cool how . . . those different connections can be made.

In an even further connection to the local history, scurvy was also a problem with miners, the so-called 49ers, who rushed into California starting in 1848 (Nix, 2024). Working with the kitchen educators again, Stella and Julian ensure their scholars make cornbread (hopefully including the right amount of salt!), miner's pudding, and potato dishes.

Here, professional creativity stands out: have a book being read, have access to citrus through the garden because citrus is a major regional crop (both Halo and Cuties have growing and production facilities in the area), and have the resources of the kitchen. Creativity comes in synthesizing or combining these resources in new ways. The students benefit from the hands-on relationship with the food, actively participating in the reading in a way that is authentic and memorable.

As noted, citrus and almonds are two major regional crops and have both found their way into the edible schoolyard experience as representative of the local community. Likewise, the Three Sisters provide another cultural experience deeply rooted in the local community and connected historically and culturally to communities across Central and North America. The Three Sisters of corn, beans, and squash have been planted, harvested, and consumed for thousands of years and have served as staple crops deeply influencing indigenous culture (Marsh, n.d.). Also, there are biology lessons inherent to the Three Sisters, as the three plants form a symbiotic relationship where the corn provides the trellis necessary for the beans to climb, the beans help provide structure for the corn (especially in high winds, along with providing essential fertilizer), and the squash leaves help shade and cool the ground, keeping the soil moist (Marsh, n.d.). In the edible schoolyards, corn is planted with companion black beans and butternut squash, as described by Sloane, a kitchen educator:

> We talked about how they're companion plants, and they rely on each other because each one is wanting to offer something different that's going to make them stronger. And I like to relate it also to us, you know being community, like talking about the school community, and how we also rely on each other when we're making this dish, too, because it involves all of our teamwork. So, we need everyone to be engaged. Everyone should be doing something or adding something to it.

Culture and community may not show up on a standardized test but are still equally important, if not more important, skills to develop. In the kitchen, the students learn this while exploring the history and biology of the Three Sisters and while preparing farm-to-table Three Sisters tacos featuring black beans, roasted butternut squash, and corn tortillas.

References

California School Dashboard. (2023). *Home*. https://www.caschooldashboard.org/

Chapman, B. (2022, October 24). Math, reading scores show a big drop. *The Wall Street Journal*, A3.

Dietrichson, J., Bøg, M., Filges, T., & Klint Jørgenson, A.M. (2017). Academic interventions for elementary and middle school students with low socioeconomic status: A systematic review and meta-analysis. *Review of Educational Research, 87*(2), 243–282. https://www.jstor.org/stable/44667656

Grimm Family Education Foundation. (2018). *Home*. https://www.grimmeducation.org/

Harwell, M., & LeBeau, B. (2010). Student eligibility for a free lunch as an SES measure in education research. *Educational Researcher, 39*(2), 120–131. https://www.jstor.org/stable/27764564

Ilie, S., Sutherland, A., & Vignoles, A. (2017). Revisiting free school meal eligibility as a proxy for pupil socio-economic deprivation. *British Educational Research Journal, 43*(2), 253–274. https://doi.org/10.1002/berj.3260

Kiger, P. J. (2023, August 11). *How the Dust Bowl made Americans refugees in their own country*. History. https://www.history.com/news/dust-bowl-migrants-california

Marsh, E. (n.d.). *The three sisters of indigenous American agriculture*. National Agricultural Library United States Department of Agriculture. https://www.nal.usda.gov/collections/stories/three-sisters

Nix, E. (2024, January 24). *What's a 49er?* History. https://www.history.com/news/whats-a-49er

Sirin, S. (2005). Socioeconomic status and academic achievement: A meta-analytic review of research. *Review of Educational Research, 75*(3), 417–453. https://www.jstor.org/stable/3515987

Stevenson, R. L. (2016). *Treasure island*. Signet. (Original work published 1883).

White, K. (1982). The relation between socioeconomic status and academic achievement. *Psychological Bulletin, 91*, 461–481. https://doi.org/10.1037/0033-2909.91.3.461

Ylimaki, R. M. (2012). Curriculum leadership in a conservative era. *Educational Administration Quarterly, 48*(2), 304–346. https://doi.org/10.1177/0013161X11427393

CHAPTER EIGHT

STARTING AN EDIBLE SCHOOLYARD

Over the past century, school gardens, kitchens, and their combined expression as edible schoolyards have followed a pattern of birth, growth, decline, and renewal that in many ways resembles the pattern of the four seasons themselves. Dewey saw gardens and kitchens as environments in which students engage in lessons based on real-world problems, thus being authentic to the knowledge and skills needed for productive citizenship in a democratic society. The edible schoolyards were antidotes to rote learning divorced from meaningful application, a function they still promise in today's world. Likewise, Dewey's garden-centered schools formed an antidote, or alternative, to better educate the whole child in an era marked by increased urbanization and accompanying industrialization, where connections to nature were being lost in the rush to live in densely populated cities with days governed by the factory timeclock instead of the natural rhythms of daylight and sunset.

The re-emergence of garden education in the mid-20th century, much like the new growth of spring emerging from the winter chill, served as a reaction to the emphasis on science, math, and technology fueled by Cold War fears and marked by significant environmental decline as symbolized by rivers catching fire from industrial pollution. The growth of the environmental movement and the related emergence of the farm-to-table movement in the culinary world emphasized a holistic health for the environment and individuals alike. One leader in this movement, Alice Waters, used her vision for holistic health to fuel a democratic society to spark the edible schoolyard movement (Waters, 2008), which in turn formed the model for the edible schoolyards explored here. Today's edible schoolyards still grapple with the tensions between holistic and authentic education and the demands of traditional rote learning now enforced by legal mandate through standardized testing. These tensions have not fundamentally changed in the 100-plus years since Dewey laid out his vision for education.

Each emergence of edible schoolyards, therefore, represents a challenge to the status quo, and in this sense, the edible schoolyard movement promises a new story. The edible schoolyards already tell a story of educational philosophy by exploring the tensions between rote learning and child-centered learning focused on the whole child. They help to tell a story of educational history, serving as one unit of analysis through which the last century of American education can be explored. They also tell a story of pedagogical development as educators not only build edible schoolyards but decide what should be taught, learned, and evaluated within these environments. They further tell a story of educational leadership as teachers, parents, community members, and administrators envision a different way of doing education and then set about the difficult work of making their vision reality within their own school communities. This story of visionary leadership, in turn, suggests the final key story to be gleaned from the edible schoolyard experience, a story of educational reform.

The *why* of educational reform has already been explored through the history and philosophy of edible schoolyards in American education. The *how* of educational reform is another chapter in its own right. In other words, how does a leader go about effectively making lasting change in their school? Are there principles that might serve as a roadmap or a field guide to change? Modern educational scholarship has, in fact, examined the processes of effective change. Leading reformers include Andy Hargreaves who, along with Dennis Shirley (2009), promises a fourth wave of change to inspire future educational innovation that emphasizes purpose, professionalism, and catalysts for lasting change. Cohen and Mehta (2017) explore the conditions of successful change. Michael Fullan has written extensively (e.g., 1993, 2016) regarding change processes and purposes. Fullan (2016) proposes a set of principles to guide the educational reformer that includes, defining closing the achievement gap as the overarching goal, recognizing that change is socially-based and action-oriented, assuming that educators initially lack the capacity or ability to implement that change and must work to build that capacity continuously, staying the course through the challenges of change, building accountability, and establishing the conditions for the evolution of positive pressure for change.

While Fullan's work focuses on the process of educational change, his work closely mirrors findings of effective change processes from other fields, notably, that of environmental change. In a way, this is not surprising, as educational reform and environmental reform share similar characteristics. Both deal with a tension between individual needs and group/societal needs. In education, individuals need the knowledge and skills to compete in a globalized competitive society. In environmental policy, individuals need access to essentials such as clean air, clean water, nutritious food, and other life essentials. Yet in both education and the environment, an overfocus on the needs and wants of the individual can lead to inequitable use of the common resources available, with potentially disastrous effects for the community and ultimately the individuals who form that community. For example, in the environment, an overuse or hoarding of clean water resources by a few individuals may lead to thirst for people and a reduction in essential crops within the broader community. In this example, the availability of water forms a common pool resource, that is, a resource that is essential to all but may be inequitably utilized by some, resulting in a "tragedy of the commons" (Ostrom, 1990). Education faces a similar common pool resource challenge, as public schools are funded through taxpayer dollars. These tax dollars are paid by all, through various property, sales, and income taxes and should be equitably utilized within the community to ensure every student has the opportunity to succeed. Put another way, No Child Left Behind had the right idea, even if the standardized testing mandate might have moved education in the wrong direction.

Education and the environment share another challenge. In both fields, the common pool resources change over time. In education, new pressures of a competitive globalized economy have arisen and created pressures on local schools to produce students with the knowledge and skills to compete not just with their neighbors down the street, but also with their peers on different continents across the globe. A growing distrust of governmental institutions generally, and schools in particular, has led to challenges in funding, and schools face constant pressure to do more with less money. Likewise, the environment is changing with environmental impacts from one country now spreading across borders and affecting the global community. As temperatures rise and traditional weather patterns change, there is growing realization that the environment is interconnected in a globalized manner. For both the environment and education, these changes have created new challenges for a changing world. Old solutions will not work in either case. The world is not going back to the way it was.

Instead, leaders need to look forward to recognizing the changes that are occurring and seek to adapt to the new realities. Environmental studies have led to Elinor Ostrom's (1990) innovative views on how to best govern the commons within a changing world. Ostrom's adaptive governance model is most succinctly expressed in a co-authored piece (Dietz et al., 2003) that lays out five principles whose successful implementation guide effective adaptive environmental reform strategies:

1. Providing Necessary Information,
2. Dealing With Conflict,
3. Inducing Compliance, With Rules,
4. Providing Physical, Technical, and Institutional Infrastructure, and
5. Encouraging Adaptation and Change. (p. 1910)

An effective leader seeking to change their community to better adapt to the changing expectations and available resources can map their change strategy by attending to these five principles. Within the principles, there are additional suggested actions that provide further guidance. For example, encouraging adaptation and change along with providing necessary information can be accomplished by identifying interested parties (in education, this would include key stakeholders such as teachers, parents, administrators, and community members) and involving them in informed discussions, also called analytic discussions. These discussions should be collaborative in nature and focus on discussing not only the vision for change, but also the practical problems that arise along the journey of change. Dealing with conflict and providing necessary infrastructure both frequently involve expenditure of available finances. This can be addressed by establishing and using low-cost mechanisms for conflict resolution, along with utilizing the different institutions that may be involved. In an effort to establish a school garden, for example, school resources, business resources, and community resources such as grants might provide additional funding that helps reduce conflict over the allocation of available funds.

Adaptive governance is another tool that has found a home in a broad range of environmental applications and is a recognized reform strategy (Brunner, 2010; Janssen & van der Voort, 2016). More relevant to this study, adaptive governance has been utilized to examine governance of alternative and sustainable food systems (Oñederra-Aramendi et al., 2023) and experimentation within China's educational policy reforms (Han & Fu, 2022). The appropriateness of adaptive governance to adapt itself to various reform contexts is inherent to the strategy itself. Janssen and van der Voort (2016) suggest that adaptive strategies emphasize the simultaneous goals of dealing with changes while protecting the organization from becoming unstable. This is in line with the needs of educators today, especially the critical curriculum leaders who seek to challenge the standardized testing status quo but also recognize the need to provide stability for their school organizations. Too much change or change that is too fast can be ruinous for communities in general and, specifically, for the professional career trajectories of the radical leaders attempting the change. There is a difference between leadership, effective lasting change, and prophecy, pointing the way toward a different tomorrow but with little or no impact on the lived lives of actual people today.

Still, any change is going to challenge stability and may even call into question traditional views of accountability. Janssen and van der Voort (2016) ask, "Are newly arrived policies and legislations still valid? Do new services need to be developed? What is the role of our own organization?" (p.1). Critical curriculum leaders are asking the same questions. Although, with an entire generation of students now educated under the standardized testing regime started in 2001 with No Child Left Behind, the urgency of questioning the validity of legislation has long passed. Instead, critical curriculum leaders might recognize that adaptive governance, with its recognition of the tension between change and stability, is well suited to dealing with complex and uncertain changes involving many stakeholders. Further, adaptive governance's recognition that no two communities will solve the problems in exactly the same way serves as a useful guide in moving toward Dewey's vision of education.

Implementing an edible schoolyard in today's schools faces a myriad of challenges, only one of which is the challenge of linking garden and kitchen experiences with the school curriculum (Diaz et al., 2019). Concerns for health and safety, such as the proper use of knives in the kitchen and meeting local food safety standards, must be addressed. Challenges related to the use of instructional time include needing to make decisions regarding when students will use the edible schoolyards. Will time be integrated with regular classroom instruction, which in effect repurposes time originally spent on reading, writing, and arithmetic, or will the schoolyard experience be treated more as a "special," such as library time? What are the implications for other existing specials if it is treated as a special? Do the teachers and staff possess adequate knowledge to build and utilize a garden and kitchen? If not, what professional training is needed, and how will that training occur? These questions and others reveal fundamental issues school leadership must address.

Any reform attempt needs to start with leadership establishing a new vision for the future, such as the visions for edible schoolyards described and explained in Chapter 4. In adaptive governance terms, the creation of a vision involves the principles of encouraging adaptation and change along with providing the community with the necessary information needed to make informed decisions regarding that change. Rowan, a key supporter of edible schoolyard based education and president of an educational foundation promoting edible schoolyards, is particularly adept at creating and sharing a vision for edible schoolyard education and explaining the importance of experience in education: "You have to touch it in the ground; you got to plant it; and you've got to grow it, nurture it; you got to harvest it and then you got to be able to prepare it, eat it." Here, Rowan concludes a story about starting up a garden at a local elementary school. The Foundation had partnered with the school and another local community partner and tried to promote the garden vision through giveaways, such as bicycles and bags of garden produce. Rowan recounts that most of the produce was thrown away by the kids as they left. They didn't know what to do with it. So, a one-stop shop is not going to do it. Simply being given the produce is no different from not buying it at the store. Rather, it is the students' experience, the sweat equity if you will, of growing the food themselves and then being taught what to do with the food that matters. Even being given a recipe, as accompanied the bags that were tossed out did, is not enough. Again, it is the investment in the experience of cooking that makes the difference in engagement and enthusiasm. Rowan proceeds to explain that they, those involved with the edible schoolyard in this study, know what "the model looks like" for effective garden and kitchen education based on this essential vision. While the foundation does provide support, they do so only for those willing to pursue their model: "We're probably not going to be a big partner if you don't have a place to cook it and a place for students to touch it. Okay, you may have a garden program but you're not going to have an edible education program." In other words, providing the experience is key but that experience is not just going to start with a big acre-sized garden plot or a kitchen that rivals what kids might see on a cooking show on television.

The experience may start small, in seed form, so to speak, and needs to grow from there, including the development of the facilities, but also including the development of surrounding infrastructure, such as how educators will incorporate the new facilities authentically into their curriculum, instruction, and assessment. For Rowan, building administrative support forms a key part of this growth from the seed of a vision to a full-scale edible schoolyard. Here, Rowan summarizes the process he and the foundation are pursuing as they assist in the start of new edible schoolyards:

> You gotta go to the top . . . first of all, you have to kind of build the predisposition your community, and then you got to go to the top. You gotta go to the district. We have, through one of our colleagues. There's a small school up in [a nearby community]. . . . They . . . have the free and reduced lunch demographic in this small little community. And they have a school that has a space like that out there. And they want to put [in] an edible education program, and that's cool. And we put together the [partnership agreement] with them, and they map what we're doing [there.] We've got a funder who's willing to fund the first phase of this. [The Foundation] can turn them on to external funding', we can show them how to do it. They went to the superintendent, . . . gotta go to the superintendent of schools, because you've got to get their buy-in because, eventually, if this is going to be sustainable, you're going to have to show them that you can fund it for the first two years and get up and running, and you're going to have to go to the schools and get these districts to support this.

In order for edible schoolyards to work, there needs to be buy-in from those who control the schools' purse strings as there will need to be a commitment of facilities, such as land on which to place the garden, and organizational time such as, the commitment for staff to spend their time on edible schoolyard activities instead of other activities like test preparation.

Regarding developing the edible schoolyard facilities, such activity falls under the adaptive governance principle of providing physical infrastructure.

Rowan again provides insight into the funding:

> [W]hat distinguishes us a little bit is that we have grant funding from a philanthropist who funds core programs that we provide to the community through the work that we're doing. Now, anything that we want to do to expand, like the mobile kitchen classroom, those kinds of things, we have to raise that money ourselves . . . [T]hat's why we have, you know, relationships with some of the healthcare providers. Yeah, we get grant money from [a health care company]. Then from [the health care company] we've gone to both [local college and university] so that they now are connected. . . . And that's part of their sustainable future for kind of moving forward here.

Here, Rowan illustrates that while the foundation he presides over is fortunate to have a major donor sponsoring a substantive portion of the edible schoolyard activity, they still have to raise additional funds themselves. One such funding source comes from connecting with the philanthropic arm of a major local healthcare provider. Healthcare providers are obviously interested in supporting healthy activities and, like many major corporations, have funds set aside for various sized grants to show local community support.

Likewise, local universities often have their own agricultural programs that might be willing to partner in providing support. The support could be financial or in-kind type products such as seeds or compost, but could also take the form of valuable gardening knowledge. Many communities have a nearby "land grant university." Land grant universities were created by the Morrill Acts of 1862 and 1890 (the 1862 bill was signed by President Abraham Lincoln) and were established specifically to promote the teaching of practical agriculture, among other topics. The agricultural colleges themselves might be supportive of a local school's gardening efforts, or affiliated extension programs might fulfill the need. All that is required from the local school is a visionary leader willing to reach out and form the partnership.

The theme of looking for donations and grants from local sources to start an edible schoolyard is continued by Luca, the principal at one of the rural schools. Luca notes that finding the time and money for these projects can be difficult. One solution is to look for funding sources already possessed. In California, there are state-provided Extended Learning Opportunity Program (ELOP) funds. These funds can be utilized, as is the case in one of the rural edible schoolyard schools, to start an after-school club, such as the 4-H type club started for the older students at this particular school's campus.

Indeed, several of the participant schools in this study are funded by these educational enrichment funds. Local leaders might look to similar enrichment or after-school funds in their own states and districts. In addition to supporting teachers in the after-school program, the funds can be utilized to create structures such as the worm boxes, as one example. Another example of leveraging funds is described by Luca:

> This next school year is starting actually with a little pilot in summer school. . . . [We] have definitely a traditional summer school, and that's by invitation so students on IEPs that require extended school year, in addition to students that need targeted intervention, are invited to summer school. But what we're doing is we're extending that into the afternoon by offering different camp-like . . . summer camp basically . . . [experiences], but, here, free for our families. And so we're doing like a life skills [program] where . . . they will do some gardening and cooking, but they'll also do . . . money management and personal finance . . . and [learning] how to sew a button on.

Money can also be found in strange and unexpected places. A refuse collection company that serves one of the edible schoolyard communities initiated a zero-waste challenge with some prize money available. Luca speculated that the company offered the challenge thinking nobody would meet the requirements and claim the prize, but the school did, due to their recycling efforts but also due to the composting, including the aforementioned worm boxes, or worm farms, leading to an over 95% no-waste rate. The funds are recycled, pun intended, back into the garden.

Gardens are simply a well-tended collection of intentionally cultivated plants. Each of the plants starts as a seed. Likewise, as Lydia, a garden educator, advises, when starting out, start small. Acres of space to grow herbs and vegetables are nice but not needed. Start with a few raised beds. You can produce plenty that can go into salads which in turn introduce kids to new foods and, if vinaigrette dressing made with the herbs is also created, measurement and ratio lessons are involved. While starting out small, keep learning yourself, and implementing your learning with the kids.

> So just start learning by doing. Get the students involved every step of the way, and just do it. Still, learning is phenomenal, and it's worth every amount of effort that anyone's willing to put in. It's exponential, the amount

> of learning that comes from it. Like you said, in all areas—academically, social-emotional, just confidence, all those things.

Lydia continues by describing the garden's connection with the school's Positive Behavior Intervention and Support (PBIS) program. As many schools do, a student's good behavior can be recognized and rewarded with some sort of prize. At this urban school, they call these "responsibility cards," and any teacher observing a student acting in a responsible manner writes the student's name on a card, and the cards are placed in a bucket. Each Friday, a drawing is held with the winners getting their choice of some sort of small trinket. Mixed among the trinkets are packets of seeds. Some students choose the seed packets over the trinket, probably recognizing the value of the seeds to their own nutrition and the opportunity to grow food with their families, both of which build upon the confidence gained through their school garden experiences.

Many start-up gardens begin their edible schoolyard journeys with small raised garden beds formed in horse troughs. Horse troughs are readily available from many "big-box" home supply stores and other local gardening or ranching type stores. A simple galvanized steel horse trough of roughly two feet by five feet and maybe two feet or so high can be filled with dirt from the school grounds, and supplemented with compost from the same home supply store. A few herbs from the garden center, and the first garden is good to grow. Total cost can be under $100. The herbs can be used in a simple vinaigrette dressing which in turn provides a nice science lesson on emulsions.

While local businesses may be reluctant to promote tax increases or agree to other generally vague commitments of funds, many will be supportive of smaller, focused, and tangible commitments. Indeed, many businesses welcome the positive publicity and the possible tax write-offs in supporting their local schools. The first key, therefore, is to keep requests from local business clear and focused. Describe what exactly is needed and how exactly it will benefit students. In other words, encourage adaptation and change to build infrastructure by providing the necessary information for business managers to make informed decisions. The second key is to not be afraid to ask.

Valerie, a garden educator at one of the rural schools, began her journey into edible schoolyards by leveraging her husband's farming connections. She simply went to the stores where she already had a relationship through buying farm items and asked for specific items for specific purposes.

As time went on, she also leveraged Google; simply sitting at her computer, searching for, and then applying for grants from various businesses and foundations in support of gardening. While searching for grants or donations, consider a range of possibilities. Some potential funders may want to support experiential education, others might want to support an industry such as agriculture that is important to the community in their schools, others might want to support healthier lifestyles, while still others might be interested in addressing issues of food insecurity. Despite the agricultural basis of the region explored here, upwards of 40% of these students are food insecure, and that reality formed the basis for some of the initial grants received. In other words, creatively consider the various challenges and needs edible schoolyard education promises to fulfill, and seek potential funders who might be willing to address those specific needs.

When considering who to ask, also consider the school's parents. Many schools provide parents with back-to-school lists of needed supplies. Such lists often contain items such as tissues and crayons. Items like small hand tools such as trowels could be added, as could requests for gift cards to stores with needed supplies. Even gift cards to local grocery stores could be valuable in supplementing what gardens produce, especially in the early years. Like businesses, parents are more likely to provide financial support if the asks are specific, with clear connections to student learning.

Regarding culinary kitchen start-ups, again think small and simple at first and then expand as support for the experience, and the capacity of educators to effectively utilize the experience, grows. Some schools might start out with simple camping gear such as portable propane-fueled camping stoves to start simple outdoor kitchens. Other schools have utilized Charlie Carts from the Charlie Cart Project. The Charlie Cart Project provides mobile kitchens that include a convection oven, a sink, storage for utensils, pots, pans, and dishes, and an electrical power system compatible with classroom needs (Charlie Cart, 2023). Think of the Charlie Cart as a sort of Chrome Book Cart that allows the easy transportation of laptop computers from classroom to classroom but, instead, turns any space into an instant kitchen. For more information regarding the Charlie Cart Project and other potential resources, see Appendix D.

Finally, while building the physical infrastructure is important to edible schoolyard education, the adaptive governance principle of institutional infrastructure is equally important. Layla, an academic coach, encourages those starting a garden to really think about "what they want to achieve." Really, cooking or just about anything can be learned through YouTube these days. Instead, think "about the benefit of actually putting your hands in the dirt or actually teaching [students] how to properly use a knife." The emphasis here is on the real-world, hands-on, Deweyesque learning experience. Also, attend to the communication between the classroom and the gardens/kitchens. Again reflecting Dewey, the gardens and kitchens should not be isolated field trips, but rather an integrated and intentional part of the academic content students should be learning. Carson, the chief executive officer of the charter school network based on edible schoolyard education, advises searching for the "holy grail" of balance between the experiences of the gardens and kitchens and the accountability of the Common Core-based California Assessment of Student Performance and Progess tests. In his words, "If the Edible Schoolyard is detracting in any way, shape, or form [from students'] performance on the test, . . . that's a major problem."

Building the connections between edible schoolyard experiences and the academics of a typical classroom takes effort but can be done as described in Chapter 7 which highlights the why and the how of breaking down the walls between edible schoolyards and classrooms. Kylie, a principal at the urban school, talks about having the right structures supporting the right team that is willing to do the work of edible schoolyard education. Regarding the team aspect, many schools already have professional learning communities in place. These teams can leverage their collaborative professional learning time to initiate and sustain edible schoolyard education. In schools such as those in this study, where educators are hired specifically for garden and kitchen education, these educators need time to join the regular classroom teachers' professional learning communities to talk about what is happening in the edible schoolyard and to look for the natural connections with the classroom. This collaborative time forms the structures Kylie talks about and is a function of the schools' leadership.

References

Brunner, R. D. (2010). Adaptive governance as a reform strategy. *Policy Sci, 43*, 301–341. https://doi.org/10.1007/s11077-010-9117-z

The Charlie Cart Project. (2023). *Home*. https://charliecart.org/

Cohen, D. K., & Mehta, J. D. (2017). Why reform sometimes succeeds: Understanding the conditions that produce reforms that last. *American Educational Research Journal, 54*(4), 644–690. https://doi.org/10.3102/0002831217700078

Diaz, J. M., Warner, L. A., Webb, S., & Barry, D. (2019). Obstacles for school garden program success: Expert consensus to inform policy and practice. *Applied Environmental Education and Communication, 18*(3), 195–206. https://doi.org/10.1080/1533015X.2018.1450170

Dietz, T., Ostrom, E., & Stern, P. C. (2003). The struggle to govern the commons. *Science, 302*(5652), 1906–1912. https://www.science.org/doi/10.1126/science.1091015

Fullan, M. (1993). *Change forces: Probing the depths of educational reform*. Falmer Press.

Fullan, M. (2016). *The new meaning of educational change* (5th ed.). Teachers College Press.

Han, S., & Fu, H. (2022). Experimentation, policy learning, and China's education reforms. *International Journal of Educational Research, 116*. https://doi.org/10.1016/j.ijer.2022.102057

Hargreaves, A., & Shirley, D. (2009). *The fourth way: The inspiring future for educational change*. Corwin.

Janssen, M., & van der Voort, H. (2016). Adaptive governance: Towards a stable, accountable and responsive government. *Government Information Quarterly, 33*, 1–5. http://dx.doi.org/10.1016/j.giq.2016.02.003

Oñederra-Aramendi, A., Begiristain-Zubillaga, M., & Cuellar-Padilla, M. (2023). Characterisation of food governance for alternative and sustainable food systems: A systematic review. *Agricultural and Food Economics, 11*(18), 1–32. https://doi.org/10.1186/s40100-023-00258-7

Ostrom, E. (1990). *Governing the commons: The evolution of institutions for collective action*. Cambridge University Press.

Waters, A. (2008). *Edible schoolyard: A universal idea*. Chronicle Books.

CHAPTER NINE

CONCLUSION

In the spring of 2020, many schools across the country were temporarily closed as part of the public health response to the COVID-19 pandemic. The schools in this study were among those closed. Closure was not the only pandemic-induced impact on schooling. During the COVID-19 years, many states, including the one in which these edible schoolyard schools are located, also suspended the state-mandated, Common Core-based standardized testing. The school closures and standardized testing suspension emerged within the educator interviews as themes affecting the context of edible schoolyards at that time. Interestingly, not a single educator indicated they disagreed with the suspension of standardized testing. If anything, there was an underlying sense of relief at having the freedom to explore learning that more authentically addressed students' real needs regarding competence, autonomy, and relatedness through the edible schoolyard experiences.

Indeed, while nobody indicated they missed standardized testing, one teacher shared what happened as her school went into closure that spring of 2020. As the school closures loomed, she stood in front of her class and tried to explain as best she could that COVID-19 was forcing schools to close for a while, and she would not be able to see the students in person. The students also would not be coming to school, but would likely be seeing each other as class resumed via Zoom. As the reality of their changing world sunk into the students' consciousness, one little girl looked up and asked, "But, who's going to water my tomatoes?"

In one statement, this student captured what we should want in our schools: She had the competence to realize that the tomatoes would still need tending and the life cycle would continue. She had the autonomy to speak her mind related to her personal commitment to tending these living plants, a school project that authentically aligned with her values of care. She expressed the relatedness to others both as the relationship we should have with the living species in our environments (the tomatoes) and the need to work with others as part of a community (those that will water the tomatoes).

This student, like Dewey a hundred years earlier, captured the essence of what education should be: authentic to real-world situations; engaging with students' interests; developing students' growing sense of individual competence in the knowledge and skills needed for life; developing students' autonomy as unique persons with their own interests; and honoring the relatedness of employing their knowledge, skills, and values as part of a vibrant, democratic community. The first and key takeaway from this exploration of edible schoolyards is, therefore, a challenge to educators to initiate and develop experiences in their schools that likewise promote these ends. Edible schoolyards with their combined school gardens where student grow their own food and kitchens where they prepare and eat the food they have grown form one such experience. The edible schoolyard experience taps into common human needs, such as the the need for sustenance and the need to enjoy a good meal in the company of others. Edible schoolyards are accomplishing this type of education in diverse communities, including those in urban, suburban, and rural areas. Schools might consider starting small—a few planters of fresh herbs counts as a school garden—and grow their facilities and curriculum from there.

Yet, each school and each community is different. While edible schoolyards are a means of accomplishing a different view of education, they are but one means of doing so. Educational leaders should exercise their critical judgment and engage their communities in creating, implementing, and sustaining the types of authentic, engaging, and democratic activities that best support students' growth in competence, autonomy, and relatedness for their own communities.

Accomplishing this Deweyesque vision for education may require policy change. The standardized testing regime as we know it today was imposed with the passage of the No Child Left Behind legislation, which was signed into law in the first days of 2002 by then-President George W. Bush. An entire generation has now grown up living within the strictures of standardized testing accountability. Those in the generation now entering the education profession have taken these tests themselves, as students, and have not experienced an educational world without them. As an educational community within the context of American democracy, are we better off now, after a generation of standardized testing, than we were at the turn of the 21st century? The edible schoolyard experience points the way toward a more authentic, engaging, and democratic educational experience that should better serve our communities and our national democracy for the next generation. Critical educational leaders equipped with this renewed educational vision and prepared with the facts of Deweyan education's benefits should engage in the political process to effect policy change. New policy that reduces or even eliminates the narrow, rote, and ultimately inauthentic accountability mechanisms of the standardized testing regime would enable the growth of new forms of accountability better suited to our future needs.

New forms of accountability rooted in the concepts of self-determination, competence, autonomy, and relatedness might better serve the broader needs of sustaining a vibrant democracy for the next generation. Further research into what types of experiences support these goals would better equip the practitioners, policy-makers, and community leaders seeking to effect this critical change. Research into the broad impact of edible schoolyards is needed, but so is research that hones further into the details of what experiences best develop the important reading, writing, and math skills necessary for success in a capitalistic and democratic society. Further research should also focus on broader critical thinking and social skills, including the role of edible schoolyards in promoting socio-emotional learning, which is also important for relating to and functioning within a community.

Finally, the realities of standardized testing are not realistically going away any time soon. As a generation has grown up with standardized testing, it may take another generation to build the pedagogical and policy capacity to replace the current system. Educational leaders, even critical ones, for the sake of their careers and the schools they serve, must attend to the needs standardized testing creates. Further research could identify more specific connections among the edible schoolyard experiences and standards and testing needs. These findings could equip current educational leaders in their struggles to provide a better education while being accountable to the current system. At the same time, further research might also explore what authentic, engaging, and democratic opportunities are lost as educators abandon practices, lessons, and opportunities they believe are best for their students and communities in order to meet standardized testing's accountability requirements.

Everyone possessing a vision for the future and the willingness to do the work of gathering people and growing resources to make that vision a reality becomes a leader. Whether doing the practical work of implementing new edible schoolyards, reforming policy, or providing the research base to support new ideas, growing a new vision of education, like growing tomatoes, takes the engagement of critical educational leaders in building a better tomorrow.

APPENDIX A

GARDEN LESSON

THE FOLLOWING IS A sample lesson from the school garden. The 90-minute lesson occurs in late winter and provides a transition from the winter garden to preparing for the summer garden.

Garden 2/26-3/2

Ramada: (word of the day)

(Here, the students gather as a class under the ramada at the garden's center. They cover key academic concepts for the day such as necessary vocabulary. The ramada itself is about 20 feet across and built of timber from local logs. Sunscreen materials provide shade. Students sit on log benches in a circle. A portable whiteboard is used to provide written material and illustrations. Laminated cards with additional illustrations and explanations of corn, wheat, and rice are present and handed out during the discussion.)

- Staple Crops: foods that are grown and consumed in large quantities that serve as a major source of energy and nutrition
- Examples at Edible Schoolyard:
    - Carrots – immunity support, B & C vitamins
    - Onions – high in antioxidants, high in potassium
    - Kale – 1 cup = more than daily vitamin A requirement, cleans toxins
- Other Common Staple Crops: wheat, corn, beans, and potatoes. Give students a few seconds to brainstorm common produce available at grocery stores, and have them give examples.

Lesson: (side of greenhouse, possibly short garden tour)

- Recall ESY staple crops
- Talk seasonality in relation to OUR staple crops (ex. spring = carrots, brassicas, other greens; planting to harvest in summer = peppers, tomatoes, cucumbers)
- Hands-on activity options: transplant plant-starts to 4-inch pots, plant/seed a bed

Harvest: (at the garden beds, each bed about 20 feet long by about 2 feet wide)

- Monday/Tuesday = kale, cabbage, onions
- Thursday/Friday = Remove kale/broccoli/collards from beds completely

Project: (plot maintenance options)

- First, discuss the importance and key points of a healthy garden bed and why we cultivate (airflow, pest control, water absorption)
- Weed a plot (paths and beds) using tools ("Hula Hoe," hand hook) and use claws to soften topsoil
- Cultivate a bed (if available) using digging forks

APPENDIX B

KITCHEN LESSON

WE PREVIOUSLY EXPLORED EDUCATORS' favorite edible schoolyard lessons and lessons with particular connections to regular academic learning in the classrooms. This appendix provides a typical lesson as part of a kitchen experience, from start to finish, as prepared by the Edible Schoolyard Kern County curriculum director.

Noodles

Summary

In this fourth-grade lesson, students continue the instructional unit about noodles and explore different types of noodle dishes and different sauces and sources of seasoning from around the world.

Objectives

After this lesson, students will be able to:

- Prepare a soba noodle bowl with tahini sauce
- Chop, dice, and julienne vegetables
- Prepare a soft-boiled egg

Assessments

During this lesson, students will:

- Follow the recipe to completion
- Use a chef's knife to chop, dice, and julienne vegetables
- Use a timer to prepare a soft-boiled egg

Materials

For the Chef Meeting

- Soba Noodle Bowl recipe
- Ingredients and tools for recipes and demonstration
- Visual aid
- Cutting boards
- Knives
- Pot
- Timer
- Small bowls
- Large bowls

Tool Focus

- Timer

Before You Begin

- Collect all tools and ingredients and then distribute them to the tables
- Gather supplies for the Chef Meeting
- Create the visual aid
- Set out stools at the tables
- Copy the Soba Noodle Bowl recipe to hand out
- Cook the noodles
- Boil eggs and peel
- Place sanitized rags at each table

Procedures

At the Chef Meeting

1. Welcome students and let them know that we are beginning a six-lesson unit all about noodles. Share with students that noodles are a strip, ring, or tube of boiled dough, typically made with egg, flour, and oil, and usually eaten with a sauce or in a soup.

2. Ask students to share with an "elbow partner" what they know about noodles, and where they may have eaten them. Ask student volunteers to share out from their discussion.

3. Introduce the Soba Noodle Bowl recipe and ask a student volunteer to share the word of the day and the definition.

4. Ask students to wash their hands and join their table group.

At the Table

1. Meet with the table groups to introduce ingredients, review the recipe, and assign jobs.

2. Prepare the recipe.

3. Once all steps are complete, pass out job cards and assist students with setting the table. Help each student complete their task.

4. Eat, and engage students in casual meaningful conversation.

5. Have each student "bus" their own dish to proper bins in the dishwashing station.

6. Assist students in the clearing of their table and cooking station.

7. Return aprons to hooks and gather students for a closing circle.

Suggested Team Roles (Printed on Laminated Cards and Handed Out Randomly)

1. Spray – Find me beneath the sink at your cooking station (used to sanitize the table).

2. Dry – Find me at your cooking station (towels to dry the table).
3. Tablecloth – Find me at your cooking station. Ask a friend to help you cover the table.
4. Plates – How many people are sitting at your table? Will you need plates or bowls? (found at a cupboard near the cooking stations).
5. Cups – Find me at your tableware station. How many people are sitting at your table?
6. Napkins – Find me at your tableware station. How many people are sitting at your table?
7. Silverware – Find me at your tableware station. Do you need forks, spoons, and/or knives?
8. Water Pitcher – Find me at your tableware station. Fill each cup half-way.
9. Centerpiece – Find me at the centerpiece armoire (an armoire filled with about a dozen or so pre-made centerpieces from which the student chooses one for the day).

Suggested Conversation Starters at the Table

1. What do you think of this dish?
2. What would you change?
3. What flavors do you like (or do not like)?
4. Review the lesson (e.g., What is something you learned today?)
5. Make connections to home (e.g., Have you had something like this at home?)

At the Closing Circle

Thank students for their work and dismiss them from the kitchen

Word of the Day
Soba: Japanese noodles made from buckwheat flour

Connections to Edible Schoolyard Learning Targets
Techniques: boil, chop, dice, julienne, roast, whisk

Seasonality: Understand seasonality by recognizing and enjoying foods at their peak ripeness and flavor. Students know that locally sourced foods provide optimum nutritional value and support the local economy.

Connections to Standards
CCSS.ELA-LITERACY.SL.4.1B: Follow agreed upon rules for discussions and carry out assigned roles.

CCSS.ELA-LITERACY.SL.4.1.C: Pose and respond to specific questions to clarify or follow up on information, and make comments that contribute to the discussion and link to the remarks of others.

APPENDIX C

RECIPES

THE FOLLOWING RECIPES ARE used in the Edible Schoolyard Kern County's kitchens. Some are mentioned in earlier chapters as part of favorite lessons or lessons with particular connections to regular classroom work. All the recipes utilize seasonal ingredients grown in the school gardens, but the ingredients may be supplemented by other ingredients purchased at local stores.

Asian Noodle Salad

Ingredients

- 12 Cups mixed greens (spinach, chard, bok choy, kale), chopped
- 3 carrots, peeled and julienned
- 1 daikon radish, julienned
- 1 bunch green onions, sliced at an angle
- 1 bunch cilantro, chopped
- 2 Tablespoons toasted sesame seeds
- 1 lb. cooked whole wheat spaghetti

For the Vinaigrette:

- 2 limes, 1 zested, both juiced
- 2 cloves garlic, peeled and minced

- 2 Tablespoons ginger, peeled and minced
- 1 Tablespoon soy sauce
- 2 teaspoons rice vinegar
- 1 Tablespoon honey
- ½ teaspoon red pepper flakes
- 1 teaspoon sesame oil
- ½ Cup olive oil

Directions

1. In a large mixing bowl, combine all salad ingredients and toss together.
2. Make your vinaigrette: In a small mixing bowl, whisk together zest and juice of limes, garlic, ginger, soy sauce, rice vinegar, honey, and red pepper flakes. While constantly whisking, slowly drizzle in sesame oil and olive oil until combined.
3. Pour vinaigrette over salad and toss until evenly coated.
4. Garnish with sesame seeds.
5. Serve and enjoy!

Chickpea Curry Recipe

Ingredients

- 2 Tablespoons olive oil
- 1 onion, peeled and diced
- 1 Tablespoon ginger, peeled and minced
- 4 cloves garlic, peeled and minced
- 2 Tablespoons curry spice mix

- 4 carrots, peeled and sliced
- 6 potatoes, diced
- 1 Cup cooked garbanzo beans (chickpeas)
- 2 Cups (1 can) coconut milk
- 4 Cups vegetable stock
- 1 bunch greens, washed, destemmed, and chopped
- Salt and pepper to taste

Directions

1. Heat the olive oil in a large pot and add the diced onions, ginger, garlic, and curry spice mix. Sauté over medium heat for 3-5 minutes.
2. Add carrots, potatoes, garbanzo beans, and coconut milk. Bring to a simmer and add the vegetable stock. Simmer until all vegetables are tender.
3. Add the greens and season with salt and freshly ground pepper.
4. Serve with basmati rice and enjoy!

Curry Spice Mix

Ingredients

- 2 Tablespoons coriander seeds
- 8 cardamom pods
- 2 Tablespoons mustard seeds
- ½ teaspoon cumin seeds
- 1 teaspoon chili flakes
- 2 Tablespoons ground turmeric

Directions

1. In a medium-hot skillet (dry, no oil) toast the coriander, cardamom, mustard seeds, and cumin until fragrant.
2. Combine toasted seeds in a mortar and pestle, add the chili flakes and turmeric, and grind to a powder.

Dumplings Recipe

Adapted from the Edible Schoolyard Project

Ingredients

- ½ pound firm tofu, drained and pressed dry
- 1 Cup carrots, grated
- ½ Cup Napa cabbage, shredded, salted, and squeezed dry
- 2 Tablespoons green onions, minced
- 1 Tablespoon cilantro, minced
- 1 Tablespoon soy sauce
- 1 Tablespoon hoisin sauce
- 2 teaspoons sesame oil
- 2 teaspoons ginger, peeled and minced
- ¼ teaspoon pepper
- 1 package small wonton wrappers
- Asian Sauce

For the Asian Sauce

- 3 limes, juiced
- 1 Tablespoon rice vinegar

- 1 Tablespoon fish sauce
- 1 teaspoon sesame oil
- 1 teaspoon sugar
- ½ teaspoon sriracha (Asian hot sauce)

Combine all ingredients thoroughly.

Directions

1. In a large mixing bowl, mash tofu with a fork until crumbly. Add carrots, cabbage, green onions, cilantro, soy sauce, hoisin, sesame oil, ginger, and pepper. Stir until combined.
2. To assemble dumplings, place 1 teaspoon of filling in the center of each wonton wrapper, gather up the edges, and pinch to seal the dumpling.
3. Fill a large shallow pan with 1 inch of water and bring to a simmer. Set lined bamboo steamer directly in pan. Place the dumplings in the steamer, making sure they are not touching.
4. Steam the dumplings, covered, for 8 to 10 minutes until wrappers are transparent.
5. Serve with Asian Sauce and enjoy!

Creamy Mac and Cheese

Ingredients

- 1 lb. macaroni pasta
- 6 carrots, peeled and chopped
- 2 Tablespoons olive oil
- 2 cloves garlic, minced
- ½ onion, chopped

- 2 bunches leafy greens, chopped
- ½ teaspoon salt
- 1 Cup sharp cheddar, grated
- 1 Tablespoon nutritional yeast
- 1 Tablespoon heavy whipping cream
- ½ Cup pasta water
- 2 teaspoons Dijon mustard
- ½ teaspoon pepper

Directions

1. In a large pot of salted boiling water, add carrots and boil until very soft. Remove carrots from water and add pasta, cooking according to the package's directions. Drain out all pasta water, reserving ½ cup.
2. In a large sauté pan, heat olive oil over medium high heat. Add onion and garlic and sauté for 8 minutes. Add hot pasta and greens, and remove the pan from heat.
3. Place carrots in the bowl of the food processor. Add salt, cheese, nutritional yeast, heavy whipping cream, Dijon, pepper, and the reserved pasta water. Blend until very smooth. Add more water if needed to help blend.
4. Pour sauce over the hot pasta and stir until well combined. Taste and adjust seasonings.
5. Cover and let sit for 5 minutes.
6. Serve and enjoy!

Garden Salad Tacos

Recipe Adapted from Alice Waters

Ingredients

- 3 bunches mixed greens (kale, chard, spinach), chopped
- 2 carrots, peeled and thinly sliced
- 4 radishes, thinly sliced
- 2 leeks, thinly sliced
- ½ bunch cilantro, chopped
- 2 Cups monterey jack cheese, shredded
- 15 homemade corn tortillas
- 1 cup pinto beans

For the Vinaigrette

- ¼ Cup red wine vinegar
- 1 clove garlic, minced
- ½ teaspoon cumin seed, ground with mortar and pestle
- ½ teaspoon salt
- ¼ teaspoon pepper
- ½ Cup olive oil

Directions

1. Arrange tortillas on a large sheet pan. Sprinkle tortillas with jack cheese and broil in the oven until the cheese is melted (about 1 minute).
2. In large mixing bowl, toss together greens, carrots, radishes, leeks, and cilantro.

3. Place all vinaigrette ingredients into a small mason jar with a tight fitting lid.
4. Shake, shake, shake, until all your ingredients are combined.
5. Drizzle salad with vinaigrette and toss together.
6. Pile the salad onto the tortillas.
7. Serve and enjoy!

Greek Salad

Ingredients

- 3 tomatoes, diced
- 1 cucumber, diced
- ½ red onion, diced
- 1 green bell pepper, seeded and diced
- 1 yellow bell pepper, seeded and diced
- ½ Cup kalamata olives, sliced into halves
- ½ bunch fresh oregano, minced
- 1 Cup feta cheese, crumbled

For the Vinaigrette:

- ¼ Cup red wine vinegar
- 1 garlic clove, peeled and minced
- 1 teaspoon Dijon mustard
- ½ teaspoon salt
- ¼ teaspoon pepper
- ½ Cup olive oil

Directions

1. In large mixing bowl, combine tomatoes, cucumber, red onion, bell peppers, olives, oregano, and feta cheese.

2. Make vinaigrette: In small mixing bowl, whisk together vinegar, garlic, Dijon mustard, salt and pepper.

3. While whisking, slowly drizzle in olive oil until emulsified.

4. Pour vinaigrette over salad and toss.

5. Serve and enjoy!

Soba Noodle Bowl

Heat oven to 450 degrees and line sheet pan with parchment paper.

Ingredients

- 1 package soba noodles
- ½ head broccoli, chopped
- 4 carrots, peeled and diced
- ¼ Cup olive oil
- 2 cloves garlic, peeled and chopped
- ½ teaspoon salt
- ¼ teaspoon pepper
- 6 eggs
- 1 bunch rainbow chard, chopped
- ½ bunch chives, thickly sliced
- ½ bunch cilantro, chopped
- ¼ cup sesame seeds, toasted

Chef's Choice: Any seasonal vegetables can be used. Try broccoli or cauliflower in the winter!

For the Tahini Sauce

- 1/3 Cup soy sauce
- 3 Tablespoons tahini
- 1 Tablespoon rice vinegar
- 2 Tablespoons honey
- 2 limes, zested and juiced
- 1 inch piece ginger, peeled and minced
- ¼ cup sesame oil

Directions

1. First, cook the soba noodles in boiling water. Rinse in cold water, drain, and place in a large mixing bowl and set aside.
2. Next, in medium sized mixing bowl, add broccoli, carrots, garlic, olive oil, salt, and pepper and stir until well coated. Spread onto sheet pan and roast for 10 minutes or until golden brown.
3. Next, while roasting, place eggs in a pot of boiling water and set the timer for 7 minutes. Run eggs under cold water. Peel and quarter the soft boiled eggs. Place in serving bowl and set aside.
4. Next, make Tahini Sauce: In small mixing bowl, add soy sauce, tahini, rice vinegar, honey, lime juice and zest, and ginger. While whisking, drizzle in sesame oil until dressing is emulsified. Set aside.
5. Then, in large mixing bowl, combine noodles, rainbow chard, roasted vegetables, chives, cilantro, and Tahini Sauce, and toss together. Garnish with sesame seeds and boiled eggs.
6. Finally, serve and enjoy!

Indian Style Rice with Cauliflower

Before you begin, rinse rice three or four times, lightly stirring with your fingertips, until the water runs almost clear. Then soak rice in water for 30 minutes or longer.

Ingredients

- 2 Tablespoons olive oil
- ½ stick cinnamon
- 1 small onion, diced
- 3 Cups cauliflower florets, chopped
- 4 cloves garlic, sliced or minced
- 1 teaspoon salt
- 1½ Cups basmati rice
- 2½ Cups vegetable stock
- 3 Tablespoons sunflower seeds, toasted

For the Curry Spice Mix

- 8 cardamom pods, seeds only
- 1 teaspoon cumin seeds
- 1 Tablespoon coriander seeds
- 1 Tablespoon mustard seeds
- 2 teaspoons red pepper flakes
- 2 Tablespoons turmeric

Directions

1. Make the curry spice mix: Smash cardamom pods using a bench scraper and remove seeds. Throw pods away.

2. Combine cardamom seeds, cumin seeds, coriander seeds, and mustard seeds in small skillet. Toast over medium-high heat until fragrant.

3. Transfer to mortar and pestle, add red pepper flakes and turmeric, and grind into a powder.

4. In Dutch oven or large soup pot, heat vegetable oil over high heat. Add cinnamon, curry spice mix, and onion, and sauté until slightly caramelized, about 5 to 6 minutes.

5. Add cauliflower, garlic, and salt, and sauté for another 3 to 4 minutes. Taste and adjust seasonings to your liking.

6. Add the rice and vegetable stock and cover the Dutch oven. Bring to a boil, and then reduce heat to low and let simmer until the rice is done, about 10 to 15 minutes.

7. When the rice is cooked, fluff with fork, transfer to platter, and garnish with sunflower seeds.

8. Serve and enjoy!

Vegetable Chow Mein

Ingredients

- 8 ounces dried chow mein noodles
- 3 Tablespoons canola oil
- 2 Tablespoons fresh ginger, peeled and minced
- 3 cloves garlic, peeled and minced
- 2 carrots, peeled and sliced
- 2 leeks, sliced
- 1 head bok choy, chopped
- 5 ribs celery, sliced
- 3 Tablespoons soy sauce

- 3 Tablespoons honey
- 2 teaspoons toasted sesame oil
- ¼ teaspoon red pepper flakes
- 1 Tablespoon lime juice
- 1 bunch cilantro, chopped

Chef's Choice: Any seasonal vegetables can be used! Use your favorites!

Directions

1. In a large saucepan, cook noodles in boiling water for four minutes. Drain and run under cold water to stop cooking process. Set aside.
2. In small mixing bowl, whisk together soy sauce, honey, sesame oil, and red pepper flakes.
3. In wok or large skillet, heat canola oil over high heat. Add ginger and garlic and cook for 30 seconds.
4. Add carrots, leeks, bok choy, and celery and cook for 7 minutes.
5. Add noodles and sauce to wok and cook for 2 minutes.
6. Stir in lime juice.
7. Taste and adjust seasonings to your liking. Does the dish need more soy sauce, honey or lime juice?
8. Transfer chow mein to serving platter and garnish with cilantro.
9. Serve and enjoy!

Shakshuka

Ingredients

- 3 Tablespoons olive oil
- 1 pepper, stemmed, seeded, and minced

- 4 green onions, sliced
- 4 cloves garlic, minced
- 2 chard leaves, chopped
- 4 tomatoes, diced
- ½ Cup water
- 4 Tablespoons herb combination (oregano, thyme, chives), chopped
- 1 teaspoon salt
- 10 eggs
- 1 Tablespoon parsley, chopped

Directions

1. In large skillet, heat olive oil over medium heat. Sauté pepper and green onions for 2 minutes.
2. Add garlic, chard, and tomatoes. Sauté for five minutes.
3. Add water, herbs, and salt. Bring to a simmer and cook for 10 minutes. With a potato masher, gently smash tomatoes.
4. Crack eggs evenly over sauce. Cover with lid and cook for 5 minutes, until yolks cook.
5. Garnish with parsley.
6. Serve and enjoy!

Three Sisters Tacos

Heat oven to 450° and line sheet pan with parchment paper.

Ingredients

- 2 Cups summer squash, cut into ¼-inch cubes
- 2 Cups fresh or frozen corn, kernels cut off cob if fresh

- 1 red onion, diced
- 4 Tablespoons olive oil
- ½ teaspoon salt
- 2 teaspoons chile powder
- 1 teaspoon whole cumin seed, ground in mortar and pestle
- 1 Cup black beans, cooked and drained
- 1 lime, juiced
- ¼ Cup cilantro, chopped
- 5 radishes, diced
- 1 Cup queso fresco, crumbled
- 15 Corn tortillas (can use homemade or store-bought)

Directions

1. In large mixing bowl, mix squash, corn, red onion, olive oil, salt, chile powder, and ground cumin together.
2. Spread squash mixture onto lined sheet pan and roast in the oven for 10 minutes, or until caramelized.
3. In small mixing bowl, mix black beans, lime juice, and cilantro together.
4. Top each tortilla with small amount of beans and squash mixture.
5. Garnish each tortilla with a sprinkle of radishes and queso fresco.
6. Serve and enjoy!

Fun Fact

The Three Sisters, corn, beans, and squash, not only are a type of companion planting in the garden, but they also make up a complete protein. Which means, when you eat the three together, you are consuming a balanced, nutritious dish of complimentary nutrients, including carbohydrates, fiber, and protein, virtually eliminating the need for meat.

Zucchini Roll Ups

Ingredients

- 8 medium zucchinis

Cheese filling

- 15 ounces ricotta cheese
- ¾ Cup parmesan cheese, grated
- 2 eggs
- 1¼ teaspoon herbs (oregano, basil, rosemary, marjoram, chives, thyme, sage)
- 2½ Cups mozzarella cheese, grated

Sauce

- 25 ounces tomato sauce
- 1¼ Tablespoon olive oil
- 1¼ Tablespoon balsamic vinegar
- 1¼ teaspoon herbs (oregano, basil, rosemary, marjoram, chives, thyme, sage)
- 3 garlic cloves
- 1½ teaspoon salt

Directions

1. Roast sliced zucchini with olive oil, salt, and pepper to taste for 15-20 minutes.

2. In medium mixing bowl, mix together tomato sauce, olive oil, balsamic vinegar, herbs, minced garlic, and salt.
3. Spread ¾ Cup of the sauce on the bottom of a baking dish and save the remainder for later.
4. In mixing bowl, stir together ricotta cheese, parmesan cheese, eggs, and herbs.
5. Spread cheese filling on a flat zucchini slice and sprinkle mozzarella cheese on top. Roll up tightly and place sideways in the baking dish. Repeat for all the zucchini slices.
6. Top the zucchini with the rest of the sauce and sprinkle mozzarella over all of them.
7. Bake for 10 minutes; garnish with basil.

APPENDIX D

RESOURCES

The Charlie Cart Project
https://charliecart.org/

Edible Schoolyard Kern County
https://esykerncounty.org/

The Edible Schoolyard Project
https://edibleschoolyard.org/

The Edible Schoolyard Project, Berkeley
https://edibleschoolyard.org/berkeley

Fork Farms
https://www.forkfarms.com/

Grimm Family Educational Foundation
https://www.grimmeducation.org/

Grow Your Lunch
https://www.growyourlunch.com/

AUTHOR BIOGRAPHY

Michael Szolowicz has served as principal, assistant principal, and social studies teacher in comprehensive public high schools where he focused on developing literacy across the content areas, promoting critical thinking, and developing inclusive communities. He currently teaches in the Doctoral Program in Educational Leadership, Educational Administration, and Curriculum and Instruction programs at California State University, Bakersfield. His research has focused on political resistance to educational reform efforts, specifically, the efforts of parents and educators to legalize opting out of state-mandated standardized tests and the role superintendents play in statewide teacher job actions. He has published in *Educational Policy Analysis Archives, SOJO Journal: Educational Foundations and Social Justice Education, The Teachers College Record*, and *Educational Administration Quarterly*. His research interests include exploring the intersections of educational reform, politics, leadership, democratic schooling, pedagogy, and philosophy.

Foreword Contributor Biography

Dr. John Stark is in his twenty-fifth year of service as both an administrator and a faculty member at California State University, Bakersfield. He has served in various campus leadership positions, including Chair of the Academic Senate and several Senate Committees, as Director of the Doctoral Program in Educational Leadership, as Department Chair of Management & Marketing, as Associate Dean of the School of Business & Public Administration, and twice as Interim Dean for the School. Stark entered academia after sixteen years of practical experience in small and medium-sized organizations, in both the private and public sectors. After receiving his PhD in Business Administration from the University of Missouri at Columbia, his primary areas of instruction have been organizational behavior, small business management, and managerial skills. He has taught in undergraduate, masters, and EdD programs, earning the rank of Emeritus Professor of Management along the way. His research is in the development of trust, conflict resolution, and pedagogy, and he serves as an Associate Editor for the Journal of Management Education. Stark is also a consultant for area organizations in strategic planning and the development of managerial skills.

INDEX